Bobby Orr

Bobby Orr: My Game

with **MARK MULVOY**

Special photography by **HEINZ KLUETMEIER**

A Sports Illustrated Book

LITTLE, BROWN AND COMPANY
Boston   Toronto

Sports Illustrated Books
are published by
Little, Brown and Company
in association with
Sports Illustrated Magazine

LIBRARY OF CONGRESS CATALOGING IN PUBLICATION DATA

Orr, Bobby, 1948–
    Bobby Orr: my game.

    "A Sports illustrated book."
    1. Orr, Bobby, 1948-   2. Hockey.   I. Mulvoy,
Mark.
GV848.5.07A32   796.9′62′0924 [B]   74-14685
ISBN 0-316-66490-1

FIRST EDITION

Published simultaneously in Canada
by Little, Brown & Company (Canada) Limited

PRINTED IN THE UNITED STATES OF AMERICA

For My Family

ACKNOWLEDGMENTS

The idea for this book project was born in a coffee shop at Metropolitan Airport in Detroit on the morning of January 2, 1970. Bobby and the Bruins were flying to California, I was returning to New York, and as we were having breakfast Bobby suddenly said: "Let's do a book someday." Orr was only twenty-one years old at the time and, as I remember, he had a black eye, compliments of an errant hockey stick. "You're not old enough to have your life story written yet," I said to him. "I'm not talking about that," he said. "I want to do an instructional and tell people how I play hockey."

Bobby, though, wanted to wait a few more years before putting his words on tape and ultimately on paper. Finally, in January of 1973, he decided that the time was right for the first detailed explanation of how he plays the game of hockey. I told Bobby that I needed a captive Orr when we sat down with my trusty tape recorder and suggested that we wait another six months and do most of our work at his hockey camp. In writing golf instructionals with Jack Nicklaus, Gay Brewer, and Julius Boros and a curling instructional with Ernie Richardson, I had always refused to work with them at the scene of a tournament or a bonspiel. And now I did not want to work with Bobby during the hockey season because I knew his mind would be preoccupied by games, travel schedules, and the rigorous demands that always seem to intrude upon his private life.

So late in July of 1973 I took my tape recorder, two dozen cassettes, a supply of new batteries, and a list of more than twenty-two hundred hockey questions and flew to visit Bobby at the Orr-Walton Sports Camp in Orillia, Ontario. Bobby lives in a cottage on a promontory of Lake Couchiching, about a ten-minute boat ride from the camp. Each day we worked a few hours in the morning; broke for lunch, a swim, a sauna, and some instructional sessions with the youngsters at the camp; and then returned to the recorder for about ninety minutes before dinner. When Bobby finally ran out of explanations and answers after filling both sixty-minute sides of almost twenty cassettes, I returned home and began to break down the tapes. Many of his answers and explanations naturally left more questions in my mind, so I returned to the cottage for more skull sessions. As it turned out, we did not complete the taping portion of the project until the Saturday after Thanksgiving. And Bobby and I worked on the actual manuscript for the next several months.

Besides Bobby, of course, there were countless other people who contributed great time and great effort to the project. Certainly the book would not have gotten off the ice without the counsel of Alan Eagleson, Bobby's attorney, adviser, and designated penalty killer. Charles Everitt, the Little, Brown editor who still plays hockey once a week in a no-lift league for men with weak ankles and weaker backhands, tightened the manuscript by deleting 374 howevers and 258 alsos. Tom Ettinger, a sailor who works on what writers like to call "the other side" at *Sports Illustrated*, was the chief anchorman and the unsung hero as he coordinated the complicated picture-taking sessions, initiated many of the design ideas, overspent his unlimited budget and, in general, steered the work on a smooth course.

Doug Orr, Sr., Bobby's father, took me on a delightful tour of Parry Sound, Ontario, while Arva Orr, Bobby's mother, provided anecdotal and biographical material that her son had forgotten to mention on the tapes. And Bill Watters, the director of the Orr-Walton Sports Camp, helped with technical counsel about some of the intricacies of hockey.

Others who helped included Ms. Patricia O'Connor, who somehow read between my deletions and arrows and typed the final manuscript; attorney Joseph M. Cassin, who knows a whereof from a whereas; physiotherapist Karl Elieff; floater Bob Haggert; Fran Toland of the Harvard University Athletic Department; Tim O'Sullivan of Harvard's Watson Rink; co-captain Mark Noonan and goaltender Larry Ward of the Harvard hockey team; Jim Gilligan, who turned ashen-faced during a picture-taking session when one of his shots cracked against Bobby's left ankle and left him limping; L. David Otte; Sara Hill; Managing Director Harry Sinden of the Boston Bruins and his chief aide, Tom Johnson; trainers Dan Canney and Frosty Forristall and equipment manager Wally Smith of the Boston Bruins; and Tommy Kelly.

Special thanks also must go to a number of tolerant people at *Sports Illustrated*, particularly Senior Editor Ken Rudeen, Managing Editor Roy Terrell and former Managing Editor Andre Laguerre. And to photographer Heinz Kluetmeier, who didn't know the true meaning of "cold feet" until he spent seventeen consecutive hours setting up his equipment at Watson Rink.

Finally, I probably would never have finished the project on schedule without the encouragement of my wife Trish, who always refused to tell Charles Everitt that I was out of town for six weeks whenever he called to check on my progress. More importantly, she kept Kelly, Kristen, and Mark Thomas out of my office while I worked.

Mark Mulvoy
Rye, New York
May 1, 1974

I stand in for Orr as Heinz Kluetmeier adjusts his strobe equipment at Harvard's Watson Rink.—M. Mulvoy

TABLE OF CONTENTS

Acknowledgments   7

Introduction   13

Chapter One: How It Goes   39

Chapter Two: Skating   61

Chapter Three: Stickwork   83

Chapter Four: Shooting   105

The Game in Color   125

Chapter Five: Attacking   147

Chapter Six: Defense   191

Chapter Seven: Coach's Corner   227

Picture Credits   239

INTRODUCTION

Bobby Orr was four years old when Gene Fernier, a friend of his father's who worked for the Canadian Pacific Railroad, bought him his first pair of skates. Real ice skates, mind you, not double-runners. "Those skates were so big on Bobby's little feet that we had to stuff the ends of the boots with old paper," Bobby's father, Doug Orr, remembers clearly. "He wore the same skates for a couple of years until he grew into them. You know, I don't think he ever had a new pair of skates that really fit him until he was maybe fourteen years old." Even at that tender age of four Robert Gordon Orr got a late start on his hockey career. Most of his friends around Parry Sound, Ontario, had started skating out on the Seguin River—or at Bob's Point on the sound itself—when they were barely three.

Hockey is an inescapable way of life in Parry Sound, a sleepy town of sixty-five hundred year-round residents situated on Georgian Bay about one hundred and fifty winding miles north of Toronto. As the large sign atop a hill on the main highway leading to town brags to the world, Parry Sound is the "Home of Bobby Orr." The winters in Parry Sound are so long and so harsh that some of the old people in town like to joke that summer means two months of poor skating on the Seguin. The temperature often drops to forty degrees below zero during the winter months, causing the ice on the Seguin to freeze three and four feet thick, and the average annual snowfall totals more than six feet some years. "In the mornings," Doug Orr recalls, "some parents would shovel the snow from one section of the frozen river and make an open-air rink so the kids could skate after school." Snow aside, the worst part of the Parry Sound winters is the bit-ing boreas that make skating up-ice a Herculean task and flatten even the strongest trees, leaving them hanging limply toward the south.

When the Seguin eventually thaws and the pickerel begin to bite, Parry Sound becomes the prosperous hub of the rich tourist and vacation region known as the Thirty Thousand Islands of Georgian Bay. The town's winter population is more than sextupled during the short summer season, and on rainy days in July and August there are always long lines waiting outside the coin-operated laundromats on Charles and Gibson streets. The richest people in Parry Sound live up on Belvedere Hill, which offers the best pure view of the sound. Bobby Orr worked on the hill one summer as a bellhop at the old Belvedere Hotel.

Like the great majority of families in Parry Sound, the Orrs—Doug, his wife Arva, and their five children: in descending order of age, Patricia, Ron, Bobby, Penny, and Doug, Jr.—have always lived on the other side of the tracks, down across the cold, black railroad trestle that runs through the town and partially blots its naturally picturesque landscape. For a short time the Orrs shared an old duplex on River Street that was only a fifty-yard walk to the Sequin, but for most of Bobby's growing-up years they lived in a nine-room white stucco house on Great North Road snuggled in a cove against the base of Tower Hill. Standing in the Orrs' living room, family and friends could look out past a railroad spur line and a rickety freight shed and see the Seguin empty its clear water into the sound.

Doug Orr, a trim man who stands an even six feet, weighs one hundred and ninety pounds, and owns a powerful set of forearms, is only three years older than Gordie Howe. In his days as a hockey player Doug was recognized as one of the two best skaters in Parry Sound. The other was Pete Horeck, his linemate on the town's junior team. "I think I was pretty good," he says proudly. He was so good, in fact, that in 1942, shortly before his eighteenth birthday, the Boston Bruins tried to sign him to a professional contract. "I was all set to try out with the Bruins," Doug says, "but I lost interest when they told me they were going to send me to the Atlantic City Seagulls, one of their farm clubs, for some experience." Declining Boston's offer, he signed on with the Royal Canadian Navy instead and spent the war years serving on board corvettes performing convoy duty on the North Atlantic corridor between St. John, Newfoundland, and Londonderry, Northern Ireland. Although Doug had planned to resume his hockey career at the conclusion of the war, he was a family man then—having married the former Arva Steele of Callender, Ontario, the town where the Dionne quintuplets were born—and needed the security of a steady paycheck. "It was too late for me," he says ruefully. "Sure, I think I could have made it. Pete Horeck played in the National Hockey League for eight years.

The tow-headed tyke is Bobby at the age of eighteen months, while the smiling man in the Bruins jacket is Doug Orr, Sr.

The view from the Orrs' home on River Street as they looked out at the Seguin River, the happy hockey ground for all the Parry Sound youngsters.

I'll tell you, I could skate as well as Pete Horeck, if I do say so myself."

Returning home to Parry Sound, Doug took a job crating dynamite for Canadian Industries Ltd., a firm that manufactures high explosives, and went about helping his wife raise their family. As it developed, one unusual benefit of Doug's dynamite job was the fact that he worked the long night shift for many years and consequently could spend some of his daytime hours watching his son Bobby chase after a hockey puck on the Seguin. Bobby had been named after Doug's father, who was a professional soccer player in Ballymena, Ireland, before he immigrated to Parry Sound, and Doug immediately sensed that Bobby had inherited some of his grandfather's natural athletic ability.

The main event every afternoon on the ice was an endless

game of keepaway involving the kids from Parry Sound and the
Indian boys from Parry Island, who used freshly cut saplings for
their hockey sticks. In keepaway Parry Sound-style, the idea
was to take the puck from some other player and try to keep it
yourself for as long as possible. No holds barred, of course. Tow-
headed Bobby, the smallest kid on the ice, always seemed to have
the puck on his stick. "I never realized how talented Bobby was,"
Arva Orr admits, "but Doug knew it right away and wasn't afraid
to say so. Me? I guess I don't know a hockey stick from a broom-
stick." Doug laughs when he thinks about those days back in the
early 1950s. "Bobby was pretty smart for such a little guy," he
said. "He used to skate for an hour or so until his face was all
numbed from the cold. Then he'd skate off the ice, walk across the
street on the toes of his blades, and stand next to our stove for

five or ten minutes—or until he was halfway warm. We would say to him, 'Bobby, haven't you had enough for today?' but before we could get the words out of our mouths he'd be out of the house and on his way back to the ice."

Bobby's career in organized hockey actually began when he turned five and automatically became eligible to play in Parry Sound's Minor Squirt League program. He progressed through the various leagues—Squirt, Peewee, Midget and Bantam—with unique double leaps. "According to the rules," Doug Orr said, "if you were on, say, the Squirt All-Star team, then, at the invitation of the coach, you could also play for the Peewee All-Stars. It seems odd, I know, but Bobby always played for two different all-star teams." Doug Orr cannot pinpoint the exact moment when he realized that Bobby had completely committed himself to his hockey career. He thinks, though, that Bobby was at least nine—or maybe ten.

By that time the Orrs had moved to the stucco house on Great North Road. During the frigid winters Doug always closed off the living room and the adjacent family room to save on heating costs, and the Orrs rarely used the drafty garage because they rarely owned an automobile. "You never needed a car in Parry Sound those days," Doug said, "because everything was always right around the corner. We only lived a quarter of a mile from the middle of town." Rather than let the garage sit empty, though, Bobby converted it into a private shooting gallery. Let Doug Orr explain:

"Bobby had a steady routine he put himself through during the year. In the winter he would put on his skates and go play hockey on the river or the sound until darkness. We'd call and call and call, and then he'd finally come home and have his dinner. In the off season he'd go down to the garage and practice his shooting for forty-five minutes or an hour. Nailed to the back wall of the garage was a piece of wood he had cut to the exact size of a goal— four feet high and six feet wide. However, the garage was only maybe twenty feet long at the most, so he'd open the swinging doors, push them aside, and then stand out on the sidewalk—or even the street—and shoot pucks against the wall. They weren't ordinary pucks, I want you to know. No, I had hollowed out the middle of the pucks and inserted some lead filament, and they weighed about twice as much as the regular pucks. If the sidewalk or the street were not smooth enough, Bobby would shoot the pucks off a piece of plywood. Sitting upstairs in the kitchen, we all could tell how accurate his shots were by the sound of the pucks hitting the wood. If the sound was a constant thud-thud-thud, we knew he was shooting on the net. If the thuds came after some dull hums, then we knew he was having a bad time. All I know is that the nights were never very peaceful until he stopped shooting.

Trains to and from the Canadian prairie rumble through Parry Sound at all hours. Downtown is a sleepy place in winter but a teeming tourist center during the sumer season.

19

"Of course, shooting and skating weren't enough. During the off season, he would bundle himself up in a sweatsuit and then take off on a fast two-and-one-half-mile run around the hill. He never ran during the day, only at night. He never said why he did it that way, but I'm sure he was pretty self-conscious about it. He didn't want the other people in town to know how serious he was about hockey. He used to run a lot with Neil Clairmont, who lived down on River Street, and sometimes they'd go off with our dog Rex, a big Labrador. Trouble was, Rex used to get in fights along the way. Come to think of it, Bobby was pretty smart about his running, too, because he always ran wearing a very heavy pair of tan work boots. When Bobby finished his nightly run, he'd go back into the garage, shut the doors, and then lift weights for maybe twenty or twenty-five minutes. I'll tell you, he never had any trouble getting to sleep those nights."

Despite all that physical exercise, Bobby was smaller and slighter than most of his young friends in Parry Sound, standing only five feet two inches and weighing just one hundred and ten pounds in full uniform when he was twelve years old. In those days the biggest and roughest players were put on defense, with the smaller skaters assigned to the forward lines. "As I remember it, Bobby played on the wing for part of a season when he was nine or ten but then moved permanently back to the defense," Doug Orr said. "I never understood why he did it; I guess he just liked it better. One day I went to Bucko McDonald—the

The Orrs lived for many years in this stucco dwelling on Great North Road, hard by the railroad tracks. Bobby practiced his shooting in the garage, usually behind closed doors. At the right, Bobby is the skinny kid who didn't let the fish get away.

old NHL player who coached most of the all-star teams in town—and told him I thought Bobby should be playing at center or on the wings. Bucko just shook his head. He said something like 'Bobby was born to play defense,' and I never brought the subject up for discussion again." There was little doubt that Bobby was the best young hockey player in Parry Sound; so good, in fact, that in 1960 McDonald invited twelve-year-old Bobby to play with the Bantam All-Stars, a team composed mainly of fourteen-year-old skaters.

Bobby dominated the Bantam games, controlling the play from his position on defense, and Parry Sound participated in the Ontario Bantam single-elimination playdowns. With Orr playing splendidly, the Parry Sound Bantams quickly qualified for the championship game against a team from Ganonoque, a town on the Saint Lawrence Seaway about three hundred miles from Parry Sound. Although Bobby hardly realized it at the time, the National Hockey League's long courtship of Robert Gordon Orr began in that game at Ganonoque.

There were only six teams in the NHL at that time, and according to league rules they could sign scrubbed-faced kids such as Orr to what could be lifetime contracts once they reached the age of fourteen. Once an Orr, say, signed his Junior A (amateur) card with an NHL club, that same organization owned his professional rights as well. Therefore, to ensure a steady flow of good young talent to their junior hatcheries, all NHL teams scouted twelve- and thirteen-year-old hockey players with tremendous care. If a scout happened to discover a twelve-year-old right wing in, say, Smooth Rock Falls, Ontario, who had better moves than Gordie Howe, he immediately wired an emergency report on the young prospect to his NHL front office. Two days later a half-dozen members of that team's top brass suddenly would appear in Smooth Rock Falls to scout the player themselves. If they concurred with their scout's assessment, they then offered a sum of money to the organization in Smooth Rock Falls that sponsored the amateur hockey program. While this financial gesture did not legally bind any player in Smooth Rock Falls to that NHL club, it did establish a debt of sorts that the NHL team hoped would be cashed in when the player reached his fourteenth birthday.

And so it was that the Montreal Canadiens, the Toronto Maple Leafs, and the Detroit Red Wings all dispatched one of their scouts to cover the various Bantam playdown games, while the Boston Bruins, who unquestionably were the worst team in the NHL at that time and would continue to hold that sorry distinction for the next seven years, sent a complete task force of top-level management to scout the young talent. Included in the Boston party were Weston W. Adams, Sr., the late president of the team; General Manager Lynn Patrick; Coach Milt Schmidt; and top scouts Harold "Baldy" Cotton and Wren "Bird" Blair. The Boston brass ostensibly was at Ganonoque to scout—and hopefully sign—two fourteen-year-old prospects on the Ganonoque team named Higgins and Eaton. In order to scout Higgins and Eaton with professional perspective, the Bostonians decided to scatter themselves throughout the stands in the small Ganonoque rink but agreed to meet between periods at the coffee stand and compare their notes.

Blair, Schmidt, and Patrick all vividly remember their instant initial impressions of Orr that night. "As soon as I saw this little kid in droopy pants from Parry Sound running the game, I quickly forgot about Higgins and Eaton," said Blair, who used to be the general manager of the Minnesota North Stars. "When we met after the first period, all five of us talked about only one player. Orr." Schmidt, who later became Boston's general manager and now runs the new Washington, D.C., franchise in the NHL, recalled that "Bobby's pants were so big, they hung below his knees, and the sleeves on his jersey looked long enough to

23

reach the ice. Still, he was in complete control of what was happening on the ice. He reminded me of Doug Harvey of the Canadiens. Harvey owned the puck when he was on the ice, and Orr did, too." Patrick, who is presently the senior vice-president of the St. Louis Blues, also was awed by Orr's command of the activity in the game. "There were players in the NHL," Patrick said, "who couldn't feather a pass the way Orr did that night—and Orr was only twelve years old. He always caught his teammates in stride and put the puck right on their stick. He was amazing. He could have played for the Bruins that year without embarrassing himself at all."

As it turned out, Orr—easily the smallest player on the ice—played fifty-eight of the game's sixty minutes that night (he spent the other two minutes in the penalty box) and left the Boston scouts totally spellbound. Mainly because of Orr's outstanding play, Parry Sound won the championship game over Ganonoque 2 to 1. After the game the Boston management group caucused in Ganonoque to plot its next move. The meeting was very brief. Adams affixed his signature to a check for one thousand dollars, gave it to Blair, and promptly sent him off to Parry Sound with orders to donate the money to the town's amateur hockey program. Out of the goodness of the Bruins' hearts, of course. Of course.

In 1962, Parry Sound was the capital of the scouting world

Understandably, Parry Sound was the capital of the scouting world the next two years as the NHL anxiously waited for Orr to reach his fourteenth birthday. Besides his scouting duties with Boston, Blair also coached the Kingston Frontenacs in the Eastern Professional Hockey League. To keep in constant touch with the Orrs, Blair oftentimes detoured the Frontenacs through Parry Sound on their travels through Ontario. Scotty Bowman, who was a junior coach for Montreal then and now coaches the Canadiens, dropped by Parry Sound so frequently that he practically became eligible to vote in the town's elections. Crafty Bob Davidson of the Toronto Maple Leafs took the intellectual approach, visiting Orr's school principal and his teachers and trying to persuade them to convince Orr that his best future educational opportunities were in Toronto—and no place else. Orr played for several teams in Parry Sound during those two years, and for every game the seats were always packed with NHL scouts.

In 1962 Orr finally turned fourteen and became eligible to sign his standard Junior A card. Bowman, of course, wanted Orr to sign with the Canadiens and play for their team in Peterborough, Ontario. Davidson implored Bobby to sign with Toronto and play in Toronto, right there in Maple Leaf Gardens. The Detroit Red Wings told Orr he would love living and playing for their team in Hamilton, Ontario, while the Chicago Black Hawks tried to convince him that there was no city in Canada quite like Saint Catherines, Ontario. Blair, meanwhile, offered Bobby the choice of playing for the Niagara Falls, Ontario, Flyers or for Boston's new Junior A team in Oshawa, Ontario, a city twenty-five miles east of Toronto. More importantly, though, Blair included a significant compromise in his offer.

Blair had established a solid rapport with the Orr family, and he correctly sensed that Arva Orr was not wildly enthusiastic about the idea of her fourteen-year-old son moving away from Parry Sound and living in a strange city with a strange family. In Junior A hockey the players on, say, the Oshawa Generals move into Oshawa and board in with local families from September through the middle of June. They attend regular school classes during the day, or at least they are supposed to, and then they either practice or play a game at night. The typical Junior A schedule includes some fifteen preseason exhibition games, approximately sixty league contests, and then as many as twenty-five postseason play-off matches. As a result, the young players spend long days and longer nights in buses traveling throughout Ontario and even into Quebec. For their services, Junior A players receive no more than sixty dollars per week, from which they must pay their room, board, and other expenses.

Mrs. Orr is a fiercely determined but quiet woman who treats her children equally. Once a reporter called the Orr residence in Parry Sound and asked Mrs. Orr if he could speak to her son. "Which one?" she said coolly. "I have three sons." Luckily for Boston, Blair understood Mrs. Orr's attitude, so he suggested to the Orrs that the Bruins would be willing to let Bobby commute from Parry Sound to either Niagara Falls or Oshawa for his first year. No practices. No meetings. Just the games. If, of course, Bobby was good enough to make the roster at either Niagara Falls or Oshawa. When Blair proposed that stay-at-home plan to the Orrs, Mrs. Orr smiled warmly and nodded her head approvingly. Still, the ultimate decision belonged to Bobby.

"My wife and I always tried to let the kids make their own decisions," Doug Orr said. "As concerned parents, we pointed certain things out to them and stressed certain good or bad angles about a situation, but we always let them make the final choice.

Bobby worked at Adams's Men's Store and spent most of his paycheck buying new clothes. Brother Doug, Jr., standing with Doug, Sr., works there now and he, too, spends his paycheck on new clothes.

I knew Bobby was only fourteen years old, but he was mature for his age—and we both felt he deserved to make up his own mind. After all, he'd have to live with that decision for a long time, maybe the rest of his hockey career."

Bobby wrestled with the decision for more than five months. "I forget whether he worked down at Adams's Men's Store or at my brother Howard's butcher shop on James Street that summer," Doug Orr said. "That's a laugh. He used to spend all his profits buying clothes or buying steaks. He decided to quit working for Howard because one day he severely cut the knuckle of his left thumb trying to slice some bacon. Anyway, at five o'clock every afternoon he was either sitting in a boat out on the sound or standing near the rapids on the river with a fishing rod in his hands. I used to go out with him a lot, so did Neil Clairmont. We'd be out there four and five hours, and sometimes we wouldn't exchange more than a dozen words. Bobby was always like that.

You could look at him and tell that he was lost in his thoughts."

At the end of the summer Bobby finally reached his decision, and on Labor Day of 1962, with his parents sitting alongside him, he signed his Junior A card with the Boston Bruins on the kitchen table of the Orrs' residence on Great North Road. Besides the unique commuting plan that Blair had proposed, the agreement between the Bruins and the Orrs also called for a twenty-eight-hundred-dollar bonus—one thousand dollars in hard cash, nine hundred dollars for a new stucco job on the family home, and nine hundred dollars for a secondhand automobile that, it turned out, never was bought. The Orrs, instead, bought Bobby a nine-hundred-dollar Canada savings bond. The Bruins also promised to buy Bobby some new clothes if he made the team at either Niagara Falls or Oshawa, but later they conveniently forgot about that.

Why the Bruins? Why not the Canadiens, who were the annual champions of the NHL in those years, or the Maple Leafs, who were only a hundred and fifty miles away, or the Red Wings, or the Black Hawks? "Bobby always wanted to do things *now*," Doug Orr said. "He always watched the NHL games on television, but he never listened to them. He knew, though, that the Bruins were really down and that they'd probably stay down for a long time. He figured he had his best chance with Boston, that's all there was to it. And also, in the back of his mind he knew that the Bruins had been donating some money to the hockey program in Parry Sound. So why not sign with Boston? It sure looked to be the quickest way to the NHL."

A few days later Doug and Arva took Bobby to the railroad station in Parry Sound. "The Bruins were holding their Junior A tryout camp at Niagara Falls," Doug said, "and we told the conductor to make sure that Bobby made all the right changes and everything. To be honest about it, we both thought he was just going there for a week's holiday. He was only about five feet five and weighed but a hundred and twenty-seven pounds—and, of course, he was only fourteen years old. We figured they'd take a couple of looks at him and then tell him to come back in another year or two—after he grew up. I never dreamed he'd make it down there." However, despite his family's private doubts and his obvious lack of size, Orr clearly was as good as even the most experienced eighteen-year-old defensemen at that camp in Niagara Falls. After two weeks the Bruins asked Bobby where he preferred to play during his junior career: Niagara Falls or Oshawa. The Niagara Falls team was very established, filled with holdover players from the previous season, while the Oshawa club was relatively new to the Ontario Hockey Association. "He picked Oshawa right off," Doug said. "I was glad for that because Oshawa is two hours closer to Parry Sound."

When Bobby phoned home to tell his parents that he would be

commuting to Oshawa all year, they were understandably speechless. And also unprepared for the hectic activity that marked their days for the next eight months. "It was almost a three-hour drive to Oshawa," Doug said, "and, of course, it was a three-hour drive back to Parry Sound. I used to borrow cars, or get friends such as Bob Holmes to drive Bobby and me to Oshawa, or wherever it was that the Generals happened to be playing. Bobby would sleep about half the time on the way to the game. After the game we'd all pile right back into the car and head home. He used to sleep all the way back to Parry Sound. The roads were pretty bad in the dead of winter. We hit a lot of snowstorms, and there was ice everywhere. Most nights we never got home until around three in the morning."

Arva Orr remembers how her son used to wait ever-so-impatiently for the time to come for his ride to Oshawa. "He always sat in a chair and tapped a ruler or a pencil," she said. "After a hundred or so taps the noise would get to me and I'd tell him to stop it. So he'd stop the tapping and walk up and down the street instead. Was he nervous? No. I'd say he was more anxious than nervous. He had something to do, and he wanted to get it done."

Although Orr was easily the youngest of all the players in the Ontario Hockey Association, he had a splendid rookie season and somehow managed to score 21 points for Oshawa. "Considering the long car trips for every game and his lack of size, I never understood how he did so well," Doug said. "Arva and I both knew, though, that he shouldn't have to spend another year trying to play hockey under those conditions. He was fifteen years old when he went back to Oshawa for his second season, and we both realized he was old enough and mature enough to handle the responsibility of living away from home. If he was going to be a hockey player—and God knows that's what he wanted to be—then we had to let him be a hockey player and live in Oshawa. It was tough on Arva and the girls at first, but they got used to it. Bobby used to call home once a week or so, and I could always tell when he was on the phone because someone would be crying."

Whenever the Oshawa team had a break of several days in the schedule, Bobby would surprise his family by suddenly appearing at the front door with a suitcase in his hand. "I'm glad he never called to say he was coming home," Arva Orr said, "because I would have worried too much. It scared me to think he was hitchhiking from Oshawa all the way to Parry Sound. Sometimes he'd get rides to the end of town and then walk the rest of the way. Other times he'd get a ride right into town. I remember one day I was in town doing errands and ran into a friend of mine. She told me her husband had picked Bobby up on the highway a couple of nights before and driven him home.

At fourteen, Bobby was the youngest player in the junior-level Ontario Hockey Association when he skated at defense for the Oshawa Generals in 1962.

Most times I didn't know who picked him up, and to tell you the truth, I'm glad I didn't."

Although Bobby resided in Oshawa the next three seasons, Doug Orr still drove down for most of the games—leaving Parry Sound at 4 P.M. after working all day at Canadian Industries, arriving in Oshawa shortly before game time, departing for home around 10:30 P.M., and then reaching Parry Sound about 2 A.M. On occasion he had to miss some of the Oshawa games, so his sister, Mrs. Margaret Atherton, who lived near Oshawa, took his place in the stands and provided vocal encouragement for her nephew. One night she went beyond that when a rival player named Chuck Kelly crashed Bobby into the boards, right below where she was sitting. "Brute," she screamed at the unsuspecting Kelly, then she slapped him on the forehead as her nephew skated harmlessly away.

Orr scored 29 goals in his second year at Oshawa and 34 in his third, then led the undermanned Generals to the Ontario championship in his final season. Along the way he continued to work with weights, and by the time he was finishing his junior career he stood five feet ten inches and weighed a strong and solid

one hundred and sixty pounds. As champions of the Ontario Hockey Association in 1966, the Generals automatically qualified to play for the Memorial Cup, to select the top junior hockey team in Canada. Before each cup game, there were large advertisements in all the Toronto-area newspapers. Some of the ads cried: "SEE BOSTON'S $1,000,000 PROSPECT BOBBY ORR." Others simply threatened: "PROBABLY YOUR LAST CHANCE TO SEE BOBBY ORR PLAY JUNIOR HOCKEY." Unfortunately for Oshawa, Orr injured his groin during the Memorial Cup finals. He tried to play on practically one leg, but Oshawa lost the series.

Meanwhile, back in Boston, the Bruins were suffering pain greater than a sore groin. It was 1966, of course, and the lowly Bruins had not made the NHL's Stanley Cup play-offs since 1959. Nevertheless, the Boston fans were not terribly distressed over the sick condition of the Bruins. Weston Adams and his publicists had already convinced the people in New England that once Bobby Orr arrived in Boston, the Stanley Cup would follow almost immediately. So after every Bruin loss, the fans simply consoled themselves under the Boston Garden in watering spots like the Iron Horse and dreamed about the hope for tomorrow — not the disaster of the past.

Then one day Hap Emms, the elderly general manager of the Bruins, put the First Coming of Bobby Orr into a fresh perspective. The Toronto Maple Leafs, it seems, had offered the Bruins a reported 1.5 million dollars for the professional rights to Orr. Emms publicly scoffed at the Maple Leafs. "We wouldn't trade Bobby Orr for 1.5 million dollars and all the players on the Toronto hockey team," Emms stated emphatically. "Orr will make the Boston franchise a winner and keep it that way for years."

On that note, enter Alan Eagleson. In the summer of 1953 Eagleson, having just completed his sophomore year at the University of Toronto, took a position as the recreation director for MacTier, Ontario, a small town twenty-five miles south of Parry Sound. In the summer of 1963 Bobby Orr was the regular shortstop (good hit, no field) on the MacTier junior team that won the Ontario championship. Late that summer Alan Eagleson, now a sharp young lawyer in Toronto, was invited back to MacTier to present the junior team with its various awards, plaques, trophies, and windbreakers. In his accompanying speech, Eagleson touched on the complexities involved in the real sports world of 1963, using the NHL — the only league known to most people in Canada — as his example. He talked about the one-way contract negotiations between management, which generally had a battery of lawyers at its disposal, and players, who usually approached salary discussions without any legal or financial advice. He mentioned how the NHL had broken up the league's first players' association by exiling some of its founders, like Ted Lindsay, from Detroit, a perennial contender for the Stanley Cup, to Chicago, a perennial contender for last place. He disclosed that hockey players made less money and still were treated worse than the athletes in every other major-league sport. What Eagleson said, in effect, was that the sharp businessmen in the NHL were taking advantage of the youth of Canada — and that it was time to stop such practices.

Doug Orr was in the audience with his son Bobby, and as he listened to Eagleson he found that he agreed with most everything the lawyer said. Later that night Doug cautiously cornered Eagleson in the banquet hall and asked if he would like to handle the legal and financial affairs of his son the hockey player. Eagleson was understandably noncommittal at the time, since Bobby was only fifteen years old and hardly needed Eagleson's professional advice yet. Doug Orr let the matter slide for two

Ian Young was the most promising young goaltender in Canada when he played with Bobby in Oshawa. Unfortunately, his dreams of a great NHL career ended one night when he stopped a Mickey Redmond shot with his eye.

more years, but when Bobby was playing his final season in Oshawa he went to see Eagleson again and convinced the lawyer to accompany him to one of Bobby's games. Obviously amazed at the proficiency of young Orr, Eagleson immediately agreed to represent Bobby in his contract negotiations with the Boston management that summer.

Hap Emms of the Bruins apparently was unaware of the liaison between the Orrs and Eagleson when he contacted Doug and Bobby early in the summer of 1966 and offered eighteen-year-old Bobby a two-year contract with the Boston team for the standard U.S. dollars that NHL clubs always gave to grateful rookies. The average salary in the NHL then was less than fifteen thousand dollars per season, while the normal starting salary for a rookie was less than eight thousand dollars. The Orrs listened politely and attentively as the sixty-one-year-old Emms went through his long and windy spiel about "what the Bruins are doing for you, Bobby, by offering you this kind of contract to play in the National Hockey League." When Emms finished his prepared speech, he started to reach for a contract, figuring that his remarks had totally wowed the Orrs. It was then that the Orrs referred him to Eagleson.

Orr's contract ushered all hockey players into a new era

Emms was totally taken back by their unexpected response and muttered that he would never have anything to do with a lawyer in his contract negotiations with players. His adamant stance recalled the position that Vince Lombardi, the late coach and general manager of the Green Bay Packers and later the Washington Redskins, had taken one year when Green Bay's all-pro center Jim Ringo surprised Lombardi by bringing along his lawyer-agent to his annual salary conference in Lombardi's inner sanctum. "You don't mind if he's here with me, do you, Coach?" Ringo asked Lombardi. "No, not at all," Lombardi answered. "Just wait here a minute. I'll be right back." Lombardi left the room for five minutes, then returned. "Now about that contract for Mr. Ringo this year," said Ringo's agent. Lombardi half laughed and half scowled as he interrupted the man. "If you want to discuss Mr. Ringo's contract," Lombardi said, "then you'd better call the Philadelphia Eagles. I traded

Mr. Ringo to Philadelphia five minutes ago."

As the Orrs and Eagleson knew, Emms was in an untenable position. The Bruins had promised the people in Boston and all New England that eighteen-year-old Bobby Orr was coming to save their franchise, so they had to sign him—or else. Still, Eagleson was in no rush to resume negotiations with Emms. As a matter of fact, he told the press there was an excellent chance that Orr might pass up Boston's offer and sign with the Canadian National Hockey Team instead. If the Bruins thought that the Orrs and Eagleson were simply playing a waiting game with Emms, the talk of Bobby's possible involvement with the National Team rudely awakened them.

Stung by Eagleson's words, Emms promptly reopened his negotiations with the Orrs *and* Eagleson, only this time he adopted a more conciliatory posture. There were meetings at the Orrs' residence on Great North Road, at Eagleson's law offices in Toronto, and also on board Emms's yacht, which was docked at Barrie, Ontario, a city about a hundred miles south of Parry Sound. Finally an agreement was reached, and at 2:30 A.M. on Saturday, September 3, 1966, Bobby Orr signed his first professional contract with the Bruins on a table in the stateroom of Emms's yacht in Barrie. It was a two-year contract that also included a signing bonus, and the total U.S. dollars involved came to a reported seventy thousand. By NHL standards at that time, Orr had broken the bank. As it developed, Orr's rich contract as well as his steadfast refusal to bend under pressure from the antiquated system known as the NHL ushered all hockey players into a new and prosperous era.

With Orr in tow, Eagleson soon organized the first official NHL Players' Association, and hockey at last became a two-way street. Consider for a moment what Orr's actions in 1966 did for hockey players everywhere: Seven years after Orr signed that first contract with Boston, the average annual salary for players in the NHL skyrocketed from less than fifteen thousand dollars to almost fifty-five thousand dollars, an increase of almost 300 percent. Also, in 1973 mere rookies with ordinary credentials signed long-term, no-cut contracts for considerably more than one hundred thousand dollars per season. When Orr turned professional, there was not even one hockey player—not Gordie Howe, not Bobby Hull, not Jean Beliveau—who was making fifty thousand dollars a year. In 1973 the average player's salary in the NHL was fifty-five thousand dollars, and there were more than thirty pro players earning more than a hundred thousand dollars per season. True, expansion and the creation of a rival major league, the World Hockey Association, helped inflate the salary level, but as one crusty old NHL owner said one day: "None of this would have happened if Orr hadn't come around and brought that guy Eagleson." Indeed, some NHL owners and general

managers now identify the old days of hockey as "Before Orr" and call the new era "After Orr."

Shortly after signing with the Bruins, Orr reported to their preseason training camp at London, Ontario, a city of some three hundred thousand people about a hundred miles straight west from Toronto. As he checked into the Bruins' motel, Orr happened to spot Johnny Bucyk, the team's captain, standing in the lobby and immediately walked over to introduce himself. "Mr. Bucyk," he said, extending his right hand, "I'm Bobby Orr. It's very nice to meet you." Bucyk clearly was taken back by the action of the tow-headed rookie. "For a moment I thought that maybe he was putting me on," Bucyk said, "but then I realized he was serious. I told him to forget the Mr. Bucyk stuff. Heck, if what I'd read about him was even halfway right, I knew I'd probably be calling him Mr. Orr before the end of the season."

The Bruins assigned Number 27 to Orr in training camp, the same number worn by Frank Mahovlich of the Toronto Maple

Leafs. Bobby played superbly in exhibition games and proved that his press notices were hardly words of extravagant praise. When the regular season began in October, the Bruins took away the Number 27 and gave Orr Number 4. Four, of course, rhymes with Orr—as in Boston Goal Scored by Number Four Orr. As all the trivia experts now know, the Boston player who wore Number 4 before Orr was Al "Junior" Langlois, a journeyman defenseman.

Although Boston again finished in last place that season, Orr disappointed no one with his play. He successfully introduced a stunning new concept to the professional game with his frequent rink-long rushes, and some of the game's most serious thinkers suggested that Orr should be called a "rover"—not a defenseman. He scored 13 goals in his rookie season, won the Calder Memorial Trophy as the NHL's outstanding rookie, and also earned a position on the league's second all-star team. At the end of that season the venerable Harry Howell of the New York Rangers was voted the winner of the James Norris Memorial Trophy as the game's best defenseman, and in his acceptance speech Howell was very humble. "I'm glad I won this award this year," he said, "because I have a feeling that Bobby Orr will win it next year and every year until he retires."

Howell's feelings proved to be unbelievably accurate. Orr won the Norris Trophy in his second season and has won it every year since then. He also made the first all-star team in his second season and has done so every year since then. He won the Hart Trophy as the NHL's Most Valuable Player in 1969–70, 1970–71, and 1971–72. He won the Ross Trophy as the league's top scorer in 1969–70, the only time a *defenseman* has ever led the NHL in scoring. And he won the Conn Smythe Trophy as the outstanding performer in the play-offs in 1970 and 1972. Not coincidentally, Boston won the Stanley Cup—symbolic of world hockey supremacy—in both 1970 and 1972, with the ubiquitous Orr scoring the winning goal in overtime of the final cup game in 1970 and also scoring the winning goal in the final game in 1972. Here is a list of the records that Orr set or tied during his first eight years in the NHL:

1) Highest assists-per-game average, career: .925 assists per game
2) Highest points-per-game average, career: 1.313 points per game
3) Most 100-or-more-point seasons: 5 seasons
4) Most consecutive 100-or-more-point seasons: 5 seasons
5) Most assists, one season: 102 assists
6) Highest assists-per-game average, one season: 1.31 assists per game
7) Most assists, one season, including play-offs: 109 assists
8) Most goals, one season, by a defenseman: 37 goals (twice)

35

9) Most assists, one season, by a defenseman: 102 assists
10) Most points, one season, by a defenseman: 139 points
11) Most assists, one game, by a defenseman: 6 assists
12) Most assists, one period: 4 assists

Play-off Records
1) Most assists, one play-off year: 19 assists
2) Most points by a defenseman, one play-off year: 24 points
3) Most goals by a defenseman, one play-off year: 9 goals
4) Most assists, one period: 3 assists (twice)
5) Most consecutive games with points, one year: 14 games
6) Most Stanley Cup–winning goals: 2 goals

Replicas of all the awards that Bobby has ever won, as well as many of the pucks and the sticks that he used to set all those records, now rest in a large trophy case—six feet high and twelve feet wide, in the combination den-and-game room on the ground floor of a new brick home at 104 Gibson Street in Parry Sound. Bobby had the four-bedroom house built for his parents in 1971. Two years later Doug Orr, then only forty-eight years old, retired from the shipping room at Canadian Industries Ltd. after spending thirty years on the job. Now he works full-time for his son, keeping the Orr-Walton Sports Camp in Orillia, Ontario, just a seventy-five-minute hop down the road, in working order all year.

Doug and Arva Orr sat in the spacious kitchen of their new home one afternoon, and each offered a personal reflection about their son the hockey player. "I only get to see some of his games in Toronto or Buffalo," Arva Orr said, "but I remember one game in Buffalo when the Bruins scored eight or nine goals and Bobby only got one assist the whole night. Afterwards I told him he didn't work hard enough to break a sweat. You know what he told me, jokingly, of course? He said, 'Mom, I hope you enjoyed tonight's game because it was your last.'"

Doug Orr laughed as his wife finished her story. "I always thought he was fairly good," he said, "and I was certain he'd be good enough to survive in the NHL. I remember a game in Montreal a couple of years ago. He has tremendous fakes, you know, with his head and shoulders and eyes and arms and hips and legs and knees and ankles and feet all going in different directions, if you can imagine that. I always think he's going to throw himself out of joint. But this night he came down on two Montreal defensemen and gave them so many fakes that they slammed into each other and fell to the ice. Bobby went around them *easy* and beat the goaltender. Let me tell you. I never dreamed he'd be as good as he is."

Good hit, no field.

CHAPTER ONE

How It Goes

Ilived on those skates that Mr. Fernier was nice enough to buy for me. They certainly were not the hundred-and-twenty-five-dollar pro-only model skates that the kids of today think they need in order to be able to skate like so many little Yvan Cournoyers, but they were ice skates—and that's all I ever cared about. My dad had them sharpened when the blades got too dull, and my mother used to put shoe polish on the boots when they got all scuffed up. As far as I was concerned, my pair of skates was the best pair of skates in the world. Sure, they were too big for me. Sure, they did not have tendon guards and ankle guards and toeplates built into the boots. Big deal. They were *my* skates. And boy was I ever happy.

You know, kids do not need the best of everything to have fun on a hockey rink when they are only five or six or seven years old. Few kids I knew in Parry Sound ever had a new pair of ice skates that really fit them snugly until they were at least ten years old. Some of us even used hockey gloves that our fathers had used years before—and no doubt thought they had worn out. Just because hockey gloves don't have any palms doesn't mean they no longer are any good. I usually wore some heavy woolen gloves inside those old gloves to keep my hands from getting cold. And hockey sticks. We never had sticks with fiber-glass coating that were the right lie and the right height and the right weight because sticks weren't made that way in those days. Some of the sticks we used had as much tape as wood because we were always afraid they would break into pieces. We loved it.

Thinking back to those days in Parry Sound and comparing them to what I see nowadays, I realize how fortunate I was to have grown up when I did. And where I did. Everyone in Parry Sound took an active interest in hockey. When we came home from school in the afternoon, we never had to worry about scraping the fresh snow off the ice because some parents already had done it for us. Oftentimes there were more people watching us play hockey than there were kids in the game. And we never had a difficult time finding someone to coach us. Someone, that is, who knew the fundamentals of the game and, more importantly, knew how to teach them. Like how to skate. How to shoot. How to pass. How to check. And how to play your position. I always had good coaching in Parry Sound, thanks to men like Alec Eager, and they used to bring in Bucko McDonald to coach the various all-star teams.

Unfortunately for hockey, that type of interest no longer seems to exist on either side, not even in Parry Sound. There are more diversions now for the kids *and* their parents. In Parry Sound, I suspect that kids spend more time on snowmobiles now than they do on ice skates. My father tells me that you can actually count the number of people skating on the river and on the sound. It's pretty sad. The kids nowadays seem to skate only on artifical ice—and preferably indoors. What that means is simply this: they really do not get a chance to skate. Take the normal team of eight-year-old hockey players. The kids probably get two hours of ice time a week. Instead of skating the way we used to in Parry Sound, though, they scrimmage or play real games. So for every hour that a team has the ice, the average player gets on that ice for only twelve or fifteen minutes. That means he actually skates for less than half an hour each week. Back in Parry Sound we used to skate as many as thirty hours each and every week from the end of October until the middle of April.

Worse than that, interest in coaching seems to have suffered, too. Believe me, you do not have to be a super hockey man to coach a team of young kids. All you really have to know are the fundamentals. Skating. Shooting. Passing. Checking. And positional play. They are not that difficult to learn. I know many men in the Boston area who never played hockey but became good coaches simply by reading every hockey instructional book they could get their hands on. Scotty Bowman, for instance, never played professional hockey, but he has been one of the NHL's best coaches in both St. Louis and Montreal. He studied how the game should be played. It *can* be done that way.

Let me make one thing perfectly clear right here. Hockey is just a game. It is not a science or something that only a computer can play. No robots, please. Ted Williams claims that hitting a round baseball with a round bat is the single most difficult thing to do in sport. Wilt Chamberlain probably thinks that shooting free throws from the foul line is twice as difficult as hitting a baseball. And I'm certain that George Blanda believes kicking field goals with eleven monsters charging toward you is much tougher than shooting free throws. Then again, I've never read or heard any athlete in any sport say that some other game is physically or mentally tougher than his. That is only natural.

Me? I can't imagine a sport any tougher than hockey. It is the fastest team sport in the world, with the players on the ice skating along at breakneck speeds. We wear more than a dozen pieces of protective equipment during a game, but I don't know of too many players in the NHL who haven't had a few stitches sewn into their faces and bodies. What's so easy about getting crashed into the boards with a vicious bodycheck? What's so easy about getting slashed across the face by an errant stick? What's so easy about skating down-ice at full speed and trying to control a puck at the end of your stick while five players on the other team are whacking away at your body? What's so easy about throwing yourself in the way of a flying puck? And what's so easy about shooting that puck past the goaltender? Talk about pressure, consider the poor goalies. All game long we fire pucks at them. Some shots travel faster than a hundred miles per hour. The best goaltenders stop at least eight of every ten shots, yet when the odd shot gets past them a bright red light flashes to tell the crowd that the goaltender just goofed. Show me a re-laxed goaltender, and I'll show you a bad goaltender. Remember Glenn Hall, the great goaltender for the Chicago Black Hawks and the St. Louis Blues? The pressure bothered him so much that he vomited before every game.

So don't tell me that football or basketball or baseball is a tougher game than hockey. We all play tough games!

I like to watch football on television, but I am never impressed when the analysts report how smart the quarterbacks are because they occasionally call "audibles" at the line of scrimmage. A couple of times a game the quarterback brings his team to the line of scrimmage and then suddenly notices that the safetyman has turned his left foot about forty-five degrees to the outside. Well, that subtle movement by the defensive player automatically cancels the play the quarterback called in the huddle, so he audibles a new play at the line of scrimmage. That's his job. Brilliant? Maybe so, but then what word do you use to describe a hockey player? Hockey is a sixty-minute game of audibles. There are no planned plays in hockey. No bunts. No pick plays at the top of the keyhole. No flanker reverses.

Have you ever seen a hockey coach send in a play from the bench? "Okay, guys, we'll work the blue line face-off option with the right wing flaring in—on hut." Or have you ever seen a hockey coach even give signals from the bench? "Okay, guys, when I (1) scratch my forehead; (2) tug on my tie; (3) place my left hand on my right hip; and (4) blink my right eye three times

Hockey is the fastest team sport in the world—and no doubt the roughest. There is nothing quite like a good, clean bodycheck to wake you up once the game begins.

41

that means we give the puck to Esposito two feet short of the blue line." No way. Sure, there are certain things we try to accomplish when we're on the ice. For instance, in Boston we like to get the puck to Phil Esposito in the slot whenever he is on the ice, and we like to get it to Johnny Bucyk at the goal mouth to the goaltender's right side when we are on the power play. However, I can never remember myself consciously trying to set up such situations more than a split second in advance.

Hockey simply is a game of instinct and mistakes. When I am on the ice, I look for openings. That's what the game is all about. I see an opening on the ice—maybe one of my teammates has skated into the clear or maybe I know I can beat a particular defenseman because he has turned the wrong way, things like that—and I instantly react to it. Maybe I react to openings quicker than other players, I don't know for sure. When I see something that looks open to me, I go. See you later! Believe me, nothing I do on the ice is the result of any grand master plan. I never stand behind my net with the puck and decide that I'm going to skate down the right wing, cut through center at the red line, stop at the far blue line, and fire a slap shot two inches off the ice and one inch inside the near post. I simply stand behind my net and head wherever my instinct tells me to go. In football you hear a lot of television talk to the effect that "his primary receiver was covered, so he went to his secondary receiver and completed the pass." In hockey there is no one primary receiver on the ice; there are four primary receivers—all the other players on your team. I play defense by instinct, too. I see some player coming toward me, then I react instinctively. He has the puck, so what I do depends on what he does. I would look pretty foolish if I committed myself to, say, taking the puck carrier to the boards when he already had committed himself to going inside of me. I never decide—in fact, I can't decide—upon my course of defensive action until the confrontation is live, staring me in the face. Then I react.

I know that all may sound pretty farfetched, but it's true. Many times after a game I sit in the dressing room and ask myself why I did certain things that night on the ice. As a rule, I cannot even answer my own questions. I remember one night I watched a video-taped replay of the game we had just played, and I really could not believe I had done some of the things that the tape showed I had done in living color. On this one play I tried to crash between two defensemen in an attempt to get in alone on the goaltender. I never made it—I was dumped to the ice—and as I looked at the tape I thought how dumb I must have been even to try such a stupid play. Then the more I thought about it, the more I realized it wasn't such a stupid play after all. The cameras filming the game provided only a side view of the action, while down on the ice all the action was squarely ahead of me. In other

When we move onto the attack, Phil Esposito always heads for the slot and plants himself directly in front of the rival goaltender. Here he looks for a rebound after the Detroit goaltender has made a save.

words, what I saw on the ice, the cameras did not see from the press box, and what the cameras saw, I didn't see. As I remembered the play, one of the defenseman had made a move that indicated he planned to play me to go wide on him. Seeing this, I reacted by going to the inside where the *opening* should have been. He faked me out, though, and when he came back inside himself, I was in trouble. Win some, lose some.

At times it's impossible for me to explain what I do on the ice, and why I do it. I remember another game when I suddenly did something I had never done before. I had the puck in the other team's end of the ice, and there were two players checking me pretty closely. The next thing I knew, there I was all alone in front of the goaltender. I honestly did not know what I had done to get there; in fact, I was so surprised to find myself in that unguarded position that I missed the net completely with my shot. After the game I watched the video tape and discovered that I had sneaked past the defensemen by making a sudden counterclockwise circle on the ice. Well, the next day I was back on the ice at the Boston Garden to take some pictures for a promotional booklet, and the photographer asked me to "do that thing you did last night when you spun around like a top." I spent the next twenty minutes trying to re-create that move, but I just couldn't do it. So how did I do it during the game? Instinct. Reflexes. I never planned to do that move, and I certainly never consciously tried to do it. It just happened, that's all I can say.

I trust my instinct. When it tells me to take a chance and make a certain play, I never worry too much about the possible repercussions if the play does not work for some reason. I may be a defenseman, but I never take a defensive attitude into a game. As I learned when I was back in Parry Sound, hockey is one sport that tolerates mistakes. Hockey, remember, has that great equalizer—the goaltender—waiting back there to cover up a great majority of the mistakes that the forwards and defensemen make during a game. And, of course, sometimes the *mistakes* you make really aren't mistakes after all.

In 1970 the Bruins won the Stanley Cup by defeating the St. Louis Blues four games to none in the final series. The fourth game went into overtime, and shortly after the start of sudden death we shot the puck into the St. Louis zone. I promptly took my position at the right point. One of the Blues' defensemen got the puck and shot it along the boards toward my position at the point. Since it was sudden death, I should have made the safest possible play and backed out of the St. Louis zone. Without thinking, though, I darted for the puck. Mistake Number 1. If a St. Louis player had reached the puck before me, the Blues no doubt would have had a two-on-one break against us. Fortunately I got to the puck first and knocked it back into the corner to Derek Sanderson. Then I instinctively skated toward the St. Louis goal. Mistake Number 2. I should have retreated to my position on the point because it was vacant. As I cut in toward the goal, Sanderson flipped a perfect pass onto my stick, and I moved in alone on Glenn Hall. When Hall started to drop to the ice, I should have flipped the puck over him and into the net. Instead, I slid the puck along the ice. Mistake Number 3. Maybe so, but when a goaltender is falling down or moving from one side to another in his crease, he also must leave a pretty big space between his feet. My shot along the ice went between Hall's feet, into the net, and we won the Stanley Cup.

Game Day

We play ten exhibition games, seventy-eight regular-season games, and as many as twenty-one Stanley Cup play-off games during a season. Like most hockey players, I am a creature of habit from the middle of September, when we report to training camp, through the end of the play-offs in the spring.

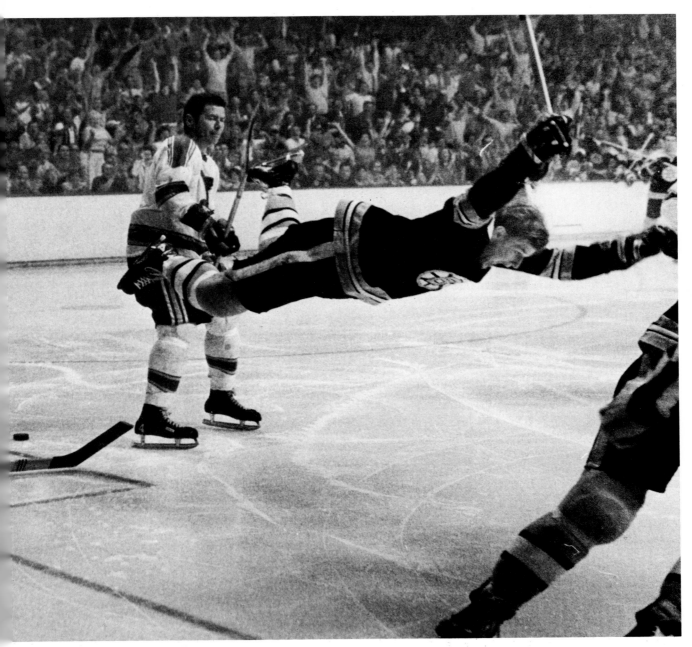

Ecstasy! This is how I looked moments after scoring the goal that beat the St. Louis Blues in overtime and won the Stanley Cup for the Bruins in 1970. Glenn Hall is the goaltender, Noel Picard the defenseman whose stick I tripped over.

When I joined the Bruins in 1966, I established my own standard routine for the day of a game—and it has not changed one bit since then.

If we have not played a game the night before, I get up around 9:30 A.M. and have breakfast, which means one egg—usually soft-boiled or scrambled—coffee with milk and sugar, and two slices of buttered toast. I love toast. In the summer I prefer dried toast for diet reasons, but during the season I don't worry too much about what I eat because of all the skating we do. If we have played a game the previous night, I don't get up until about 11 A.M.—and then I skip the egg and the toast and just have a cup of coffee. The Bruins normally do not hold team strategy meetings the morning of a game, but sometimes I go down to the Boston Garden anyway and skate for ten or fifteen minutes. If I don't go to the Garden, I take a walk or do some shopping, anything to get out and get my body in motion. Whatever I do, though, I'm always back in the apartment by noon to have my regular pregame steak.

Some of the rookies coming into the NHL nowadays amaze me with their peculiar pregame meals. Jim Schoenfeld of the Buffalo Sabres likes to eat cold spaghetti or cold ravioli right out of the can before games at home. Ugh! Although most players wait until almost 2 P.M. before having their steak—or spaghetti—I like to play on a half-empty stomach, so I eat early. I'm not a gourmet cook by any means, but I broiled some mean steaks during my first seven years in Boston. Now I've taught my wife Peggy how to broil them medium-rare, the way I like them. Sometimes I have salad with my steak, and when I have not had an egg for breakfast I usually have one with my steak.

After lunch I take a nap for about an hour—no longer. Then it's 1:30 P.M. Time to get up, get dressed, and get to the Garden. I'm always the first player to arrive in the dressing room before a game. In Boston our games start at 7:30 P.M., but I usually check into the room between two and two-thirty. I once tried staying home until 5:30 P.M., like all the other Bruins do, but I couldn't sleep or relax. In the room I work on my equipment for about thirty minutes, taping the tops of the handles of my sticks to get the feel I want (I don't like those bulky knobs on the handle) and making certain that my pads don't need any repairs and my skates have been sharpened the way I like them. To be truthful, I guess you could say that I look for things to occupy my time. I don't want to start thinking about any hockey game five hours before the first face-off. Cripes, I'd be a basket case in no time.

After a while I play gin rummy with Frosty Forristall, the assistant trainer of the Bruins and my old roommate. We have had a running game for more than seven years, and I think he leads me 67,246 points to 67,231. Someday I plan to demand a recount. We play for about an hour, then Frosty and Dan

Canney, our trainer, have to get things in order for the game, so I play a bit of solitaire and watch television: old movies, the soap operas, cartoons, anything to keep my mind off the game. Around five o'clock I get a rubdown to relieve the usual soreness in my muscles. However, if my legs still feel sluggish after that rubdown, I have Jock Semple, a master masseur and therapist, come in and rub them again. By then the other Bruins have arrived for the game, and at 6:15 P.M. I start getting dressed.

I take a good half hour to put on all my equipment, and when I finish I sit quietly on the bench at my place with a weighted hockey stick in my hands. I roll that heavy stick in my hands for about fifteen minutes, trying to acquire a feel for it—like the baseball player who swings a lead bat in the on-deck circle—so that my regular stick will feel as light as a pencil when I take the ice.

While waiting, I think about rival players and their moves

When rolling the weighted stick I also start to think about the team we are playing that night. Mind you, I never think about what I might be able to do against another team; instead, I think about rival players and the moves they like to make most often. Every player in the NHL favors a particular move when he has the puck. However, it would be stupid for me to divulge any of those particulars since I still have to defend against all those players. Say, though, we're playing the Montreal Canadiens. Almost automatically I warn myself before the game not to forget that Jacques Lemaire likes to set up house in the slot, that both Yvan Cournoyer and Frank Mahovlich like to break out of their own zone early in anticipation of a lead pass from one of their defensemen, and that Peter Mahovlich, Frank's younger brother, tends to fake a shot and stickhandle around you when he is on a rush. If we are playing Buffalo, I think about Gilbert Perreault, the great young center of the Sabres, and all his tricky shifts and head fakes, and I worry about Richard Martin, the fast left winger with the wicked shot, who usually comes down on my side of the ice. There's a highly publicized winger on one team that I never worry too much about, though, because he always makes the same move—a terrible fake to the inside, then a burst along the boards. He hasn't had any great success

against the Bruins since his second or third game against us. We go onto the ice for our pregame warm-up right after 7:00 P.M., but before we go I take my regular hockey stick and walk around our dressing room tapping my teammates on their shin pads and wishing them good luck. Then I'm ready.

What happens after the game depends on what happened during the game. If we lost, I'm ornery and get a little ugly. For seven years I always took those games home with me and never had to worry about upsetting anyone else. Now that I am married, I must learn to leave those games there in the dressing room. Win or lose, I don't sit around our dressing room too long

My friends in Philadelphia offer some encouragement (left). There are many good fans around the league, but I consider Boston's the best. They know the game and don't let us forget it.

after a game. I want to have a couple of soft drinks, get dressed, and go home. The hockey writers in Boston and in other cities complain that I am inaccessible after a game because I don't stand around my dressing place and discuss the events of the game with them. Listen. If a writer wants to ask me a question, all he has to do is ask it and I will answer that question to the best of my ability. But I refuse to sit around long after a game and wait for writers to ask their questions, and I certainly never volunteer questions or answers. That's not me. I don't want to be controversial. Believe me, I don't care to knock anyone in hockey or any other sport. If writers and other players want to knock me in print or on the air, fine for them. Remember that every time one player knocks another publicly, he usually has to eat those words for sixty minutes in the next game. I know what happened to Brad Park of the New York Rangers when he came out at the start of the 1972 Stanley Cup play-offs with a book that included a lot of cheap shots at some of the Bruins, particularly Phil Esposito. Park's words received a lot of play in the media during the play-offs, and I know that Esposito got all psyched up for the series. He didn't score any goals against the Rangers, but he had nine assists, won about 95 percent of his face-offs, and helped kill our penalties. After the series Phil said that what Park wrote in his book was Park spelled backwards. Well, I'm not going to get myself in controversies like that. Every time I think I'm so great, I try to do something by myself—and then I get beat badly. I never want people to think I'm any kind of a big shot. I have been blessed with talent, and in Boston I have been surrounded by a lot of extremely talented hockey players. So who am I to pop off about anything? And, as I'm sure Brad Park learned in 1972, why psych up the other guys? Hockey is tough enough as it is.

The Bruins

A few years ago one anonymous player in either New York or Montreal described the Bruins as "a bunch of kooks and degenerates who happen to get along together." True, we have always had great team harmony on the Bruins, but I don't buy that kooks and degenerates tag. Another time, when a magazine writer called us "a pack of wild animals," it was a lie. When the Bruins were a bad team through the early and middle 1960s, nobody ever wrote or said anything about them. Then we became a good hockey team, so they began calling us every name in the dictionary. And some names that weren't in the dictionary, too.

What I liked most about the Big, Bad Bruins, as people used to call us (actually we were the Big, Good Bruins), was that we always knew when to stop the joking and turn to the more serious matters of hockey. Let's face it, the NHL season is so long and so demanding that you cannot hold a totally serious posture twenty-four hours a day, seven days a week. Try playing in Minnesota one night, flying home immediately after the game, and then playing in Boston the next. If you do stay serious, you certainly won't win anything in May—like the Stanley Cup. Gordie Howe once told me that the Detroit Red Wings were a fun team when they were winning all those Stanley Cups in the 1950s, and I know that the Montreal Canadiens always enjoyed themselves en route to their cups.

Tell me, how could the Bruins have been such a bunch of bad actors if we practically rewrote the NHL's record books? In the 1970–71 season, for instance, we set records for (1) most points by a team in one season: 121; (2) most wins: 57; (3) most wins at home: 33; (4) most goals scored: 399; (5) most shorthanded goals: 25; (6) most assists: 697; (7) most scoring points: 1096; (8) most 50-goal scorers: 2 (Phil Esposito, a record 76, and Johnny Bucyk, 51); (9) most 20-goal scorers: 10 (Esposito, 76; Bucyk, 51; Ken Hodge, 43; Orr, 37; Johnny McKenzie, 31; Derek Sanderson, 29; Ed Westfall, 25; Fred Stanfield, 24; Wayne Carleton, 22; Wayne Cashman, 21); (10) most 100-or-more-point scorers: 4 (Esposito, 152; Orr, 139; Bucyk, 116; Hodge, 105). And one night we set another record by scoring three goals within twenty seconds against the Vancouver Canucks. We must have done something right.

As a group, though, we did have fun. Gerry Cheevers, who shared the goaltending job with Eddie Johnston, usually instigated the jokes, and he was our chief gag man. One night Cheesy gave up ten goals in a game we lost to the Chicago Black Hawks. Back in the dressing room someone asked him what had happened. "Roses are red, violets are blue, they got ten and we got two," Cheesy answered, and the room broke up. Another night he was having an argument in the room with a friend of his named Joe Monahan. Cheesy is a real horseman—in fact, he owns several horses himself and spends most of his off-ice hours at the race track—and he was trying to convince Monahan that some horse he owned was the biggest horse in the world. Monahan wasn't about to believe Cheesy, though, until Gerry finally said: "Joe, this horse is so big, the jockey needs a parachute to get off."

Cheesy probably was at his best when Mike "Shakey" Walton joined the Bruins midway through the 1970–71 season. Knowing that Shakey had once visited a psychiatrist during his turbulent career with the Toronto Maple Leafs, Cheevers had a big couch

We celebrate another victory.

placed in front of Walton's bench in the Bruins' dressing room so Shakey would feel right at home. Walton used to play along with Cheesy's gags, too, and the two of them worked out a psychiatrist-and-patient act that they used to play in hotel and airport lobbies. Cheevers would sit down in the middle of the floor, and Walton would stretch out beside him — and all the time Gerry would be writing what Mike was telling him. One day they practically stopped traffic at the Vancouver airport when we were stuck there for several hours.

Eddie Johnston was not as outgoing as Cheevers, but he picked good spots for his gags. Toward the end of the 1972–73 season the Bruins acquired Jacques Plante from the Maple Leafs, and according to all the rumors, Eddie J. eventually was headed for Toronto as payment for Plante. Eddie J. believed the rumors, which, of course, proved to be correct, so on our last trip to Toronto he went into the hockey shop at Maple Leaf Gardens and bought himself a regulation Maple Leafs jersey. He was the last player on the ice that day for practice, and when he appeared he was decked out in his Maple Leafs shirt. We all thought it was pretty funny, and the people who were watching practice broke up. I know that some of the front-office people of both the Bruins and the Maple Leafs didn't think it was anything to laugh at, though, because their faces were blank.

Phil Esposito does not joke around very much about anything, but we kid Phil pretty strongly about all his superstitions. I have never seen anyone as superstitious as Esposito. Read what he does while getting dressed before a game. To start, he stands up and winks at a red horn suspended from the shelf above his seat. Phil's grandmother gave it to him and said it would always ward off the *malocchio* — the evil eye. Esposito would rather play on double-runners with sandbags around his waist than miss his pregame wink. Sitting down, Phil pulls on a tattered black T-shirt, making sure it is inside out and backward, and then pins a St. Christopher medal to his suspenders. After that he deliberately sets his hockey stick onto the carpeted floor squarely between his outstretched legs so that the taped blade always points in a northwest direction. Then he places his black-and-white hockey gloves palms up alongside the butt end of the stick. At this precise instant Frosty Forristall appears with a container of white powder and splatters it on the blade of Esposito's stick. When Frosty finishes, Phil starts to look sharply around the room for some unlucky omen — like a turned-over paper cup or, shriek, crossed hockey sticks. Sometimes we play tricks on Phil by placing crossed sticks in a fairly conspicuous place and when he sees them, he goes completely bananas. He doesn't like the so-called kiss of death, either. Phil sat next to Derek Sanderson in our room, and before the start of the second playoff game against the Rangers in 1973 Derek casually said to him:

"Espy, you're so lucky. You never get hurt." Well, Phil looked as though someone had spent all his money, broken the blades on his skates, cracked all his hockey sticks, and stolen his red horn. "Oh no, Derek," he yelled at Sanderson, "never say that." Phil had missed only four games in his nine full seasons in the NHL, but he could have played in all four if they had meant anything in the final standings. Sure enough, though, in that game against the Rangers Ron Harris, a New York defenseman, caught Espy with a clean check at his knees and sent him falling to the ice in pain. Phil had to be carried off the ice, and he needed an operation on one of his knees two days later. Maybe he should be so superstitious after all.

Derek, of course, was not trying to psych out Esposito when he said that Phil was lucky not to have been hurt during his career. Poor Derek. He always finds himself in the middle of things. When he puts his mind to it, Derek can be one of the best centers

What is Derek Sanderson thinking? Only Derek knows — and he's not telling. For years Derek and Brad Park were bitter rivals on the ice. They now will be teammates on the New York Rangers.

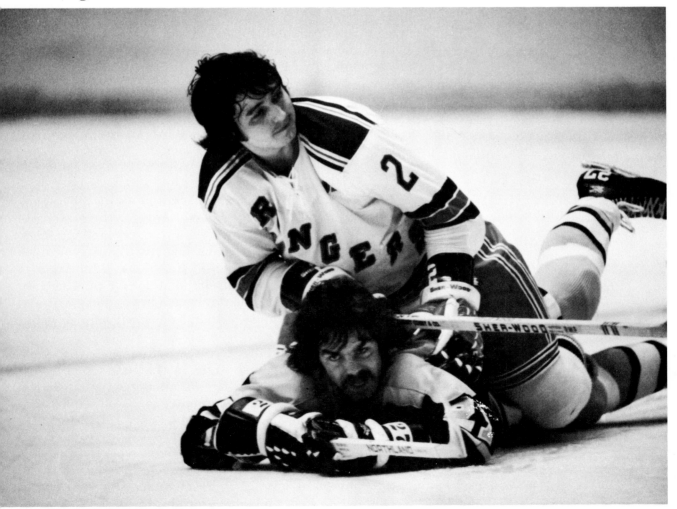

in hockey. He has tremendous talents as a penalty killer, a fore-checker, a face-off specialist, and a goal scorer. He scored 29 goals for the Bruins one year and never even played on the power play. Even Derek admits, though, that his mind has wandered from hockey the last few years. I still laugh when I think about something he did in 1973 when he returned to the Bruins after his short career in the World Hockey Association. He had bought a new thirty-thousand-dollar burgundy Rolls Royce that cost him something like eighty-five dollars just to get washed, and he had a chauffeur for it, too. One day the Rolls pulled into the rear storage area of the Garden, and when Derek stepped from the back seat he was carrying a bulky white bag with the name of a bank stenciled on it in big block letters. None of us knew what to think when he walked into the dressing room and dropped the bag in front of my place on the bench. The bag had a chain wrapped around the top—and two locks were on the chain. "It's yours," Derek told me. I didn't know if the bag had money in it—or what. Well, as it turned out, it seems that Derek and I had made a friendly thousand-dollar bet several years before about which one of us had the courage to get married first. We were both confirmed bachelors when we made the bet, but I had become engaged while Derek was playing for the Philadelphia Blazers—so he was paying off. He opened the locks, picked up the bag, and spilled the contents all over the floor. There they were: one thousand crisp one-dollar bills. Leave it to Derek. Why make out a simple check for a thousand dollars when you can give someone a thousand one-dollar bills?

My Knees

Despite what you may have read, I do not live with an ice pack wrapped around my left knee. For one thing, I won't stand still long enough to let someone wrap such a thing around my knee. For another, I simply refuse to play hockey with any type of ice pack, harness brace, or anything else on my knee. Phil Esposito wears a brace on his knee, and he claims it does not bother him during the games. Maybe I should wear a brace, too, but I like to feel nice and loose on the ice—and I know that a brace would restrict my movements.

To set the record straight, here's a summary of my knee troubles. I hurt my right knee first. In the summer of 1967 I went to Winnipeg to play a charity exhibition game. Late in the game Bobby Leiter, one of my teammates on the Bruins at the time, and I broke down the ice on a two-on-one. I had the puck, and when I dropped it over to Bobby, the lone defenseman checked me into the goal post. Before I could recover from that check, Leiter accidentally crashed into me—and I stretched the ligaments in my right knee. The doctors immediately covered my right leg with a cast, and later they determined that I would not need an operation. Still, I missed a lot of games early in the 1967–68 season while recovering from the injury. Since then, I have not had any troubles with my right knee.

I wish I could say the same thing for my left knee. I have already had three operations on that one, and I don't want a fourth operation under any conditions. My troubles all started one night during the 1967–68 season when Marcel Pronovost, a very good defenseman then playing for the Toronto Maple Leafs, caught me with a solid check as I tried to sneak past him along the boards in the Boston Garden. Ligaments. Operation Number 1. Then, late the following season, I damaged the ligaments again when my skate got caught in a rut in the ice at the Forum in Los Angeles. I played the rest of the schedule and through the play-offs, but I went under the knife during the summer. Operation Number 2. Except for the usual soreness and stiffness, I had no trouble with the left knee for the next three years. But in March of 1972, a few days before the start of the play-offs, I got hit hard—and clean—in a game against the Red Wings in Detroit—and the ligaments came undone again. The knee was terribly sore throughout the play-offs and kept swelling up. One game I had to leave our bench halfway through a period for a quick ice-pack treatment. In June of 1972 Dr. Carter Rowe of Boston cut the knee open and tightened up the ligaments. At the same time he cleaned up the insides of the knee and smoothed out the rough surfaces around the cartilage area. Operation Number 3. Some people think that bone rubs against bone in that left knee, but they're all wrong. Dr. Rowe told me there is some lubrication in there that makes the joints slide smoothly. I know that if I had not let Dr. Rowe open the knee that third time I would not be playing today. I played for a long time when the knee was sore, and it was close to unbearable. I could not play the game the way I wanted—the way I always had. In fact, I could hardly play at all. I had to have that operation. It was my only hope.

I never worried too much after my first two knee operations, but I was pretty scared after that third operation in 1972. Hockey is my life, you know, and you can't survive for long with a bad knee. When Dr. Rowe cut my knee that June, I was certain it would be strong enough for me to play at least some of the games in the Canada-Russia hockey series in September. However, when I joined Team Canada at its practice camp in Toronto it was obvious that my knee was not ready. I'd skate during practice, then afterward the knee would swell up. A couple of times some doctors in Toronto had to drain fluid from the knee. I was worried, so I called Dr. Rowe in Boston. He said not to worry, that it would get better in time. But I worried anyway. The knee was so sore that I was unable to play in the first four games of the Canada-Russia series; however, I felt extremely confident that I would be able to play in the second half of the series over in Moscow. My hopes were shattered, though, when the knee started to lock on me during Team Canada's workouts in Stockholm. The doctors decided I shouldn't play until at least the start of the NHL schedule, a month later. I tried to play at that time, but I was carrying eight or ten extra pounds and neither my left leg nor my left knee was strong enough to support the burden. So I quit for three weeks and concentrated strictly on building up the leg and the knee. I worked out at least four hours a day for those three weeks. In the morning I skated for ninety minutes, then rode an exercise bike for ten miles. After that I took a whirl-pool and got some heat treatments. In the afternoon I exercised on a mini-gym under the supervision of Gene Berde, a super physical culturist in Lynnfield, Massachusetts. I watched my diet carefully, too, and after three weeks I felt sound enough to play again. I rejoined the Bruins for a game against the New York Islanders and happened to score a goal on my first shift on the ice. I didn't miss another game the rest of that season.

Have my knees slowed me down? Yes. I definitely don't think I skate now like I used to skate, but, believe me, I'm very happy to be skating at all. People always ask me why I continue to take chances on the ice, considering the condition of my knees. I don't know why, to tell the truth. It's the way I have always played the game, the only way I know how to play the game. When I have the puck and I'm moving up the ice, I don't think about my injuries. The only thing in my mind is the goalie at the other end of the ice. You can't be gun-shy and still survive in hockey.

I pray that my knee operations are finished forever. I won't let them cut the left knee open again unless it's awfully bad inside. Hey, they've worked inside that knee three times, and there can't be much left inside there now.

Often, a good check leaves you on your knees and out of the action. When downed, you must hustle back into the play or else the other team will have a momentary man advantage.

CHAPTER TWO

Skating

Let me say it flat out right here: skating is the single most important part of the game of hockey. If you cannot skate, you cannot play hockey. It's that simple. The minor leagues are filled with young and old players who have hundred-and-twenty-mile-per-hour slap shots and whippetlike wrist shots but cannot skate the length of the rink without tripping all over themselves. If those players—and I even hesitate to call them players, since they lack the basic ingredient for being a player—had practiced their skating half as much as they practiced their shooting technique, they would be playing in the major leagues right now.

So tell me why kids hate to skate? Skate, I said, not play hockey. There's a big difference. Whenever I meet young boys at banquets and other social functions, I always ask them how they like skating. "Great," they answer, "we love to go out there and shoot the puck and throw bodychecks and get banged around." Hold it. How do they like skating. "Oh," they say after a long pause, "you mean skating, like going without the puck and doing stop-and-starts and figure eights? Gee, that's a real drag."

Skating a drag? I couldn't disagree any more. Did Jack Nicklaus think it was a waste of time when he used to huddle all bundled up in a cut-in-half Quonset hut in the middle of winter and hit thousands of golf balls onto the snow-covered fairways of the Scioto Country Club in Columbus, Ohio? Did Joe Namath and Jim Plunkett waste their time when they used to throw spirals through old tires suspended from the limbs of trees? A quarterback certainly is not a successful quarterback if he diagnoses a defense perfectly, correctly audibles for a new pass play, but then throws a dying quail thirty yards off his intended target.

And now take hockey. Once I see my opening on the ice and call my personal audible, I depend on my skating ability for the pure, basic execution of the play, just as the quarterback depends on his arm for the completion of the pass play. All my head fakes and body fakes and stick fakes and everything else will prove to be absolutely worthless if I get my skates tangled at that exact moment I instinctively break toward the opening I see on the ice.

I must confess that like most of today's young hockey players I was not aware of the great importance of pure skating when I was growing up back in Parry Sound. As kids we never consciously worked on our skating, by starting every day with a few dozen figure eights and ending with a dozen stop-and-starts. What we did—but what most kids today almost never do—was skate and skate and skate for two, four, or even five hours a day, depending on school schedules and the weather conditions. On any normal Wednesday afternoon, say, we would have at least thirty kids down at the river by two-thirty, and we would skate into darkness. We used to split up into two teams, set some goalie nets about four hundred feet apart, drop down a puck, and then chase it for hours. The game never stopped for line changes or rest periods. If you wanted the puck, you chased it like mad; when you finally controlled it, you skated like mad to retain it. Ever try skating around and through and over and under fifteen or twenty players at once? Well, that's how I learned to skate. And that's how the Russians learn to skate, too.

Forget about style, worry about results

When I was in Moscow with Team Canada in September, 1972 I happened to watch one of the Soviet junior teams working out at the Central Army Club rink on the city's west side. The regular coach of the junior team conducted a strenuous ninety-minute practice session, with forty-five minutes devoted to skating maneuvers and the other forty-five assigned to basic hockey techniques. Once that session was completed, Boris Kulagin, the tactical coach of the Soviet National Team, appeared on the ice with a portable megaphone and ordered six of the junior team players and the two goaltenders to remain on the ice. He assigned a goaltender to each net, split the six players into two teams, dropped a puck, and told them to play as though the World

62

Championship was at stake. With Kulagin screaming words of criticism at them through his megaphone, the six skaters worked feverishly for a solid hour. They paused only when someone scored a goal. When that happened, the skaters and the goaltender on the team that allowed the goal had to do fifteen push-ups on the cold ice. What the Russians did that day in Moscow, and what they no doubt do every day, was basically no different from what I used to do on the river in Parry Sound. I cannot imagine a better drill for developing a solid skating style, even including the push-ups.

As in all sports, a player's style is an individual matter. Forget about learning style. Worry about the results. In football, Namath and Plunkett set up differently and throw the ball differently. In golf, Nicklaus keeps his right hand under his left throughout the swing, while Arnold Palmer rolls his right hand over his left at impact. In basketball, Rick Barry shoots free throws underhanded, John Havlicek shoots them overhanded, and Chamberlain shoots them every way known to man. And in baseball Henry Aaron holds the bat at the bottom of the barrel and cocks his hands to hit home runs, while Felix Millan chokes up twelve inches on the handle and tries to punch the ball over second base. Now look at some of the various skating styles in the NHL.

Phil Esposito and Ken Hodge of the Bruins skate very upright and take long, powerful strides. Walt Tkaczuk also skates very upright, but his stride is maybe half as long as Esposito's. Peter Mahovlich is a combination of Esposito and Tkaczuk; he skates upright but alternates between a long stride and a short one and, as a result, most people tend to think he is a choppy skater. Dave Keon, Bobby Clarke, and Cliff Koroll all skate hunched over at various levels, with Clarke at times appearing as though his chest is parallel to the ice surface. Jean Ratelle's skating style is halfway between a Keon's and a Tkaczuk's, sort of an upright hunch, while Frank Mahovlich's style consists of a slight hunch and the longest stride in the game.

On the other hand, remember John Ferguson's style—or lack of it? Fergy was not a smooth skater by any means, but somehow he always got to the puck or to the corner just as fast as the player with the picture-book style—and he usually arrived with a bang. And what about Claude Provost, one of Ferguson's teammates with the Canadiens? Claude—we all called him Joe—was so bowlegged that you could almost throw a basketball between his legs. He had a short, choppy stride, and it always looked as though he was running after the puck, not skating after it. Running or skating, Provost was a Montreal regular for fifteen seasons. Terry O'Reilly, one of my young teammates on the Bruins, reminds me of both Ferguson and Provost. Terry is about as smooth as a stucco bathtub when he skates, but he goes

like mad once he is in gear and never keeps his arrival at his destination a secret. You know he is there.

The best skater I have ever played against is Jean Beliveau, the retired captain of the Canadiens. Tall, at six feet three inches, and unbelievably strong, at two hundred and ten pounds, Beliveau skated majestically upright and moved in long, smooth, powerful, seemingly effortless strides. By my definition he was the *classic* skater. Not ironically, I guess, since Montreal always has been the best *skating* team in the NHL, the fastest player I have ever played against also is a Canadien—Yvan Cournoyer. We call him the Roadrunner, for obvious reasons. From blue line to blue line Cournoyer probably is twice as fast as any other player in the league, with the possible exception of Jacques Lemaire. Yes, Lemaire also plays for the Canadiens. Although he is only five feet seven inches and a hundred and sixty-five pounds, Cournoyer has a pair of thighs that are as big as any other skater in hockey. He uses those muscular thighs to generate the power for his incredible standing starts. One of Montreal's favorite breakout plays, in fact, calls for the player with the puck to loft it into center ice and let Cournoyer streak between the defensemen and track it down. I suspect that the Roadrunner leads the NHL in breakaway goals each season.

I remember a game in Boston when Cournoyer absolutely flew around the rink his first few shifts and scored two goals against Gerry Cheevers. Midway through the first period there was a face-off near Cheevers, and Gerry skated out to talk with Cour-

All players have their own skating styles. Phil Esposito (left) skates upright and takes long strides, while Peter Mahovlich (right) skates upright but alternates between very long and short strides.

noyer. "Yvan," he said, "slow down, will you please?" The Roadrunner laughed. "No Ger-ry," he said in his French accent, "I have the tailwinds tonight."

There is only one Cournoyer, even in the NHL, so don't abandon your promising hockey career because you cannot skate like the Roadrunner. Who can? Instead, you should concentrate on the certain skating techniques involved with the particular position you play. Forwards, for instance, must develop quick, Cournoyer-like starts from a standing position. Besides that, they must be able to stop suddenly and reverse their direction, and they also must have a solid skating base in order to maintain their balance while getting hit with bodychecks.

As a general rule, defensemen do not have to skate as fast as forwards, since they do not skate the great distances forwards skate in such a short time. Defensemen, though, must be able to skate backward almost as well as they skate forward. Also, they must develop great turning ability. They should be able to turn left or right or backward without losing even one skating stride. Defensemen must be smart skaters. If they like to carry the puck, as I do, they must remember not to go so deep into the other zone that they will be unable to get back on defense fast enough to stop the attack once the opposition controls the puck. Despite what most people think, some of the best skaters in the NHL are the goaltenders. Watch the goaltender the next time he skates to his bench when the referee signals for a delayed penalty on the other team. He moves unbelievably fast, even though he is carrying about fifty pounds of protective equipment. When Gerry Cheevers was with the Bruins, he oftentimes challenged some of the defensemen and forwards to match races, and he won more than he lost. Cheevers once played forward for a Toronto farm team, and one year shrewd Punch Imlach tried to sneak him through the goaltenders' draft by listing him as a forward. The NHL overruled Imlach, then the Bruins smartly drafted Cheevers, and he was in goal when we won the final games for the Stanley Cup in 1970 and 1972.

Not coincidentally, the best skaters in the NHL all seem to have large thighs and what I like to call "big seats." The more you skate, the bigger you will get around the rear. Johnny Bucyk has played in the NHL for almost twenty years; his seat looks like a living-room sofa and his thighs are as thick as tree trunks. Cournoyer has about a twenty-nine-inch waistline, but his thighs are so thick and so muscled that he wears pant legs that go with a forty-inch waist. I have the same problem and must have all my pants made to order. If I bought them off the rack, I'd have to get pants with a forty-inch waistline and then have the waist taken in about six inches. Or maybe I ought to say it another way: there are few, if any, good skinny-legged skaters in the NHL.

Skates

Starting with the skates Mr. Fernier bought for me, I usually managed to get a new pair of ice skates about every three years. My father always knew I needed new skates when my toes were just about ready to pop through the boots of the old ones, and then he would go out and buy me some new ones that were three or four sizes too big for my feet. In those days a good pair of skates cost between twenty-five and fifty dollars. The price for those same skates today is between seventy-five and a hundred and twenty-five dollars, a luxury that most families cannot afford every year. Thanks to the skate exchanges that have become popular in recent years, there is no reason any more for parents to spend seventy-five to a hundred and twenty-five dollars each year on form-fitting new skates for the young hockey player(s) in the family. Skate exchanges are located in many public and municipal rinks, and they work like this: once a player outgrows a pair of skates, he takes them to the exchange, pays a nominal fee (usually no more than five or ten dollars), and then swaps his old skates for a similar pair of skates that no longer fit some other young hockey player. Maybe those exchange skates are not brand-new, but they will fit properly and, better yet, will not force parents into debt.

Be careful when you buy new skates or get a pair at the exchange. Try on several pairs until you find the skates that feel best on you. Make certain that your toes do not rub against the ends of the boots. If they do, and a puck happens to hit squarely against the toe, you will suffer terrible pain and probably even break a toe or two. In addition to that, make sure the skates have hard toes, extra protective padding near the ankle areas, reinforced inner soles, firm tendon protectors, and steady, solid blades. Some young players have trouble skating and turning because the blades on their skates touch too much of the ice surface. When I skate I touch the ice with only about one inch of each blade; the rest of the blade is my so-called "rocker." Before selecting a pair of skates, always check to find out how the blades will be for you. To do this, take one skate in each hand and hold them so that the skating surfaces of the blades rub together. If the area in which they touch is longer than an inch and a half, then you probably will have trouble skating and turning on those blades.

I wear out at least two pairs of skates each season. Once I receive a new pair, I do not just lace them on, step onto the ice, and play a game. No way. Like all players, I take great care in breaking in my new skates and acquiring a feel for the boots and the blades. First of all I take the skates and lace them on my feet very loosely. Then I put them in a tub of hot water and get them wet in order to soften the leather and make them feel comfortable. After that, I step onto the ice and practice with them for an hour or so. The next day, I go back to the dressing room and repeat everything I did the day before. When I finally finish, I wipe off the blades of the skates and hang the boots to dry. By that time, they should fit my feet perfectly. Even after all this, I still wear new skates for a number of practice sessions before I dare try them in a game.

Like most players, I want my skates to fit snugly and to feel as though they are a normal extension of my legs, so I usually wear size eight skate boots, compared to my size eight and one-half street shoes. I never wear socks over my feet, either. That way I get still a better feel for the boot and the skate. I want to control my movements when I am on the ice; I don't want to be controlled.

Unlike most players, I keep the laces on my skates tied very loosely, and I don't loop the laces through the top three holes in the boots. By keeping those three holes untied I feel I am quicker and have more agility. Nothing is holding me down. But when I tighten skates to the top hole, I feel as though my foot is in a cast, that my foot is too upright. My mobility is reduced too much. So now I tie my skate boots about as high as most people tie their shoes.

A word of caution: this may be fine for me, but I do not recommend it for young skaters. I have fairly strong ankles that have been built up by long hours of skating; however, young skaters just learning to play hockey need the ankle support that high boots laced to the top give them. There are even many pros in the NHL who need that same type of support, too. In fact, this may be a perfect example of a procedure that is good for me and most professional hockey players but very bad for the developing player. Another thing that I don't do—but you definitely should do—is to wear ankle guards around my skates because they felt clumsy when I used to wear them. To compensate for the lack of ankle guards, I have had thicker and longer tongues installed on the boots of my skates. The tongues extend to the bottom of my shin pads—and I wrap some tape around them to keep them from flapping. So I get a little extra protection without feeling too restricted. But I know I *should* wear ankle guards, particularly since I play defense.

On the ice I like my skates to be extremely sharp. The sharper your skates, the quicker you will be able to turn and the harder you will be able to push off from a standing position. I have my skates sharpened before every game and most practices, but that is hardly a necessary expense for young skaters. The sharp edge on the blade of a skate will hold for two or three good skating sessions. Maybe even longer. Alex Delvecchio of the Detroit Red Wings had his skates sharpened only once a month, and he never fell all over himself on the ice.

To determine if the blade edge is sharp, you can simply run the tip of your thumb down the blade. If the blade is sharp, it will almost cut your thumb open, so for safety's sake test the blade on your thumbnail. It should take off some of the nail's surface. Or go out onto the ice and do one stop-and-start. If you lose your footing at the start or cannot stop immediately—in other words, if you fall down—then your blade edges are dull.

We don't need skate scabbards in the NHL because we usually walk to the ice surfaces on rubber mats, and most dressing rooms have either rubber tiles or a good thick carpet on the floor. On the other hand, most public and municipal rinks offer concrete floors only. So protect the blades of your skates by keeping scabbards on them right up to the moment that you step onto the ice. Don't forget to take them off, though, or you'll fall on your head once you touch the ice.

Technique

One thing I don't understand is why so many parents insist upon buying double-runners for their children. Their feeling, I suppose, is that double-runners will provide the necessary balance to keep their little boys from falling onto the ice and getting their backsides all wet. Maybe so, but double-runners only delay the inevitable: regardless of their earlier adventures on the ice, young players certainly will fall down countless times when they finally try regular skates for the first time. I stopped counting after I fell down for the seven-millionth time on the river back in Parry Sound.

Without balance, of course, you can't skate. As tots, remember, we all learned to walk by ourselves. After a lot of false starts it came naturally. Balance comes naturally, too, after a few sessions on the ice. One way is to simply pick yourself off the ice and try to skate again each time you fall down, sort of a repeat of the way you learned to walk. Another considerably less painful way is to grab hold of a wooden chair with sliders on the legs and push it around the ice, using the chair to maintain your balance. We use this training tactic at the Orr-Walton Hockey Camp every summer. I let a skater use the chair for a day or two, then I come up behind him, talk with him for a few minutes to build his confidence, and then remove the chair from his grasp. He then is on his own and, surprisingly, usually has good control of his balance.

Once a skater has acquired basic two-legged balance on the ice, I start working with him on one-legged balance. One foot always is in the air when you are skating, right? So what I do is make a boy skate down the ice while holding his knee in the air with the handle of his hockey stick. Or I make him skate backward on, say, his left leg and keep his right leg off the ice. Oddly enough, the best way to improve your balance is to go public skating, without a hockey stick in your hands. All players use their sticks for support, and rightly so. By skating without a stick for an hour or two each week, you will gain great confidence in your ability to execute all the involved skating maneuvers in a game of hockey without falling down at the wrong moment.

As I mentioned, no two players in the NHL have the same skating style. In fact, except for Eddie Shore, I don't know of any pro coach who has tried to teach a certain skating style to all his players. Shore was a great skater and a great defenseman in the NHL during the 1920s and 1930s, and he later owned and coached the Springfield team in the American Hockey League. For some reason Shore firmly believed that players should skate with their blades exactly eleven inches apart and their backsides in a sitting-down position at all times. Shore went to extreme lengths to get his point across in practice sessions. He used to tie rope around the legs of his players and make them skate around the ice with their blades never moving farther apart than those eleven inches. After that he had them sit on folding chairs and skate around the rink.

Listen. In skating you take basic principles and apply them to the form that seems most comfortable to you. Don't copy anyone else's skating style. Phil Esposito's legs are probably five or six inches longer than mine, so his natural long stride is considerably longer than mine, too. I'd look pretty foolish if I tried to match Esposito stride for stride when we skate down the ice. Maybe I take four strides for every three that Phil takes. Maybe I take five. I don't know, to be honest. The name of the game is skating to Place A, Place B, or wherever as fast as your legs will take you there. Short strides, long strides, in-between strides, what does it matter? Getting there soon is what counts in hockey.

So here's how I skate—or try to. At times my instinct and my reflexes probably force me to skate some other way, but I am never conscious of a change. This is how I think I skate. How I hope I skate. And how I should skate.

When I am standing still on the ice, I always seem to have my feet pointing inward. Why? Comfort, I guess, or maybe it's because I am slightly bowlegged. However, if I ever tried to take off down-ice from that toes-in stance, I would trip over my feet and fall flat onto the ice. So before starting I point the front tips of my blades at right angles to the direction in which I am skating. In other words, the toes of my boots are set at about ten minutes before two o'clock. I don't look down at my feet to make certain they are positioned properly for my departure. They fall into place automatically and instinctively after years of constant practice. This stance, as you will discover, provides a strong, solid base from which to begin the actual skating process.

I am right-handed, so, in my own mind, I must be right-footed, too. Like everyone else, I have a natural inclination to do things with my so-called preferred side. I find that I have an easier time opening doors with my right hand than my left. And I always have an easier time putting my right foot forward rather than my left. Why? No reason, other than the fact that I always have preferred doing things with my right side. Consequently, I believe my right side is my power side.

So when I take off from my standing position I always lead with my right foot. The power foot. It is easier for me to lift that right foot instead of my left. For the first two or three strides, as I try to generate power from my thighs, I run more than I skate. I get up onto my toes, like a sprinter taking off in the hundred-yard dash, and lift my right skate over my left, then my left over my right, and finally my right over my left again — pushing and pushing and pushing. All this time I take short and probably choppy-looking strides, but that's the way I get into gear. Once I finish those first few strides, I come back down onto the balls of my feet and gradually lengthen my stride.

From start to stop, my skating posture remains constant. I bend my knees slightly for better balance, maneuverability, and strength on my skates. As a defenseman, I love to see stiff-legged players skating down the ice. In that posture position they cannot possibly have very good balance, so knocking them off the puck usually is an easy job. I keep my feet spread comfortably apart, though I don't know whether the gap between them is eleven inches, as Eddie Shore likes, or two feet. What's a comfortable distance between feet? Try this. Go out onto the ice, spread your feet, and do a dance. Anything. The Mop. The Flop. The Boogaloo. Even the Twist. When you can do one of those dances and still maintain a solid balance on your skates, then your feet are spread apart just right for you.

I also bend my body forward from the waist. How much? It depends on circumstances. I like to carry the puck out away from my skates, unlike a Johnny Bucyk, who carries it almost at the toes of his skates. To reach that distance I must arch my body forward into a comfortable position. Keep comfortable, and you'll always be all right. Throughout the entire skating process my weight continually moves forward in a natural manner. I

Here I am taking off from a standing position in front of the Boston goal. As you'll notice, I get a running start, push hard off my left foot, and accelerate with short, choppy strides.

Here I'm beginning to lengthen my stride. My knees are bent slightly for better balance, maneuverability and strength, and I am bent forward from my waist. Note that my head is always in front of my skates and that my body weight seems to move forward naturally—the way it should.

don't lurch—or at least I don't try to lurch. Never let your weight remain to the rear while you are skating, or else you will not have enough strength to ward off even the most ineffectual checkers. One sure way to keep your weight forward is this: always keep your head *ahead* of your skates. By that I mean your head should lead your skates into the stride. If that happens—and it should—there's no way your weight can remain to the rear.

I hope that does not sound too simple. Listen. Too many instructors introduce too many nonessential elements when they teach and talk about skating. For instance, they take an eight-year-old player and tell him to lift his feet exactly eighteen inches off the ice when he skates. What's the boy going to do? Bring a yardstick with him to practice every day? As a general rule, there is no proper height for swinging your foot while skating; it is a matter of individual preference determined by comfort and feel. What I will say, though, is that you should not lift your feet above knee level—or else you will waste valuable time and precious energy. And I don't understand why teachers tell young boys how important revolving hips are for good skating form. Despite what they say, hips are an afterthought in skating. If you work your legs correctly—that is, if you create striding power from your thighs and push off hard from the tips of your toes or the balls of your feet—then your hips will work automatically. Remember, you skate with your legs, not your hips alone.

Skating forward on a straightaway is, of course, the easiest kind of skating. Now let's discuss some of the more intricate skating maneuvers I execute in every game—such as skating backward, turning, and stopping.

Skating Backward

Like all defensemen, I move in reverse about one-third of the time I am on the ice during a game. Forwards, though, usually skate backward only when they are checking in the other team's zone, which means less than 5 percent of the time they are on the ice. Think about what I just said. Now wouldn't it make great sense if developing young defensemen spent one-third of their practice skating time working on their reverse-skating technique? Of course it would. So tell me why coaches don't split their squads during skating sessions and let defensemen and forwards practice the particular skating movements they are called upon to perform most often in a game. Unfortunately for most young defensemen, the backward skating drills usually last only a minute or two—"Okay, guys, once down the ice backward"—and are tacked onto the end of practice, almost as an afterthought. To put it bluntly, if you can't skate backward as well as you skate forward, then you cannot expect to play defense

Defensemen spend about one-third of every game skating backward. When in reverse, my knees stay forward—almost directly over the toes of my skates, and my seat lowers into a position that is practically parallel to the ice. My head also remains in front of my skates.

In this one sequence, Carol Vadnais of the Bruins demonstrates perfectly how defensemen must react to a new situation on the ice. Carol skates backward across the red line, then turns toward the puck, crosses over in the direction of the puck carrier, sets himself for a good poke check, and then stops in a strong position to collect the loose puck.

with any competence. In the late 1960s one established NHL team drafted a twenty-year-old defenseman in the first round on the recommendation of its computer, which had punched out the startling information that the boy's physical characteristics and his mental aptitude matched those for the perfect programmed defenseman. As it turned out, the perfect programmed defenseman fell on his seat every time he tried to skate backward, but then again, what do computers know about skating backward?

All right. I'm standing at the blue line, waiting for a pass-out from the corner. However, the rival team's left wing senses the play correctly, intercepts the pass-out, and starts down the ice with the puck on his stick. Do I turn around, skate like mad, stop at the other blue line, turn around again, and wait for that left wing to come to me? Never. By doing that I would lose sight of the puck for precious seconds, and maybe the left wing no longer will have it when I finally turn around. The great advantage of skating backward is that I can always keep my eyes on the puck, the carrier, and most of the other players on the ice. So when that left wing intercepts the pass-out, I start skating backward as fast as my legs will carry me.

My first move involves my seat and my knees simultaneously. I bend my knees forward so that my seat becomes almost parallel to the ice. At this point the tips of my knees are directly over—or perhaps slightly ahead of—the toes of my skates. Unlike forward

skating, to get started skating backward demands a sharp
wiggle-waggle movement with your hips in order to produce the
necessary side-to-side skating motion—consequently, your
feet should barely leave the ice at all. Also unlike forward
skating, I don't set my feet at ten minutes before two o'clock
for takeoff; for backward skating I try to set the blades parallel. Since my right foot is my preferred foot and my power
foot, I push off from the inside of the blade of that right foot and
wiggle my hips toward the left, thus creating, from my personal
viewpoint, a right-to-left motion. Depending on the length of the
stride I need at the particular time, I ultimately plant the inside
of my left blade into the ice and then continue backward by pushing off the inside of that left blade and wiggling my hips to the
right. During each stride my feet almost come together, but
never touch. Now that I think about it, I don't skate backward as
much as I weave in reverse from side to side. I keep my posture
constant—knees bent, seat parallel to the ice—throughout, and
I maintain solid balance by keeping my head in front of my skates
and never letting my body weight move too much to the rear.

One common fault I have found among young defensemen is
that they glide backward, not skate backward. There is a difference. When you glide, you do not have total control over your
movements. When you skate, though, *you* create the power, the
movement, the direction; in effect, you control what you are
doing. Never glide on the ice at all.

Turning

For some strange reason, there is not a hockey player in North America—well, maybe there's one, but I've never seen him—who steps onto the ice, takes a left turn, and proceeds to skate in a clockwise direction. If a rookie ever showed up at the Bruins training camp and tried to take a leisurely clockwise skate, he no doubt would get run over by two dozen other skaters traveling in the customary counterclockwise direction. As you might guess, hockey players are creatures of habit; the first hockey coach probably told the first hockey team to skate from right to left at its first practice session, so it became an unwritten rule and has passed through the ages. What that counterclockwise habit means, though, is that players generally experience little difficulty negotiating right-to-left turns on the ice but tend to trip over themselves or glide aimlessly while making left-to-right turns. There are three basic turns I make during a game—the circle turn around the net, the crossover turn on defense, and the tight turn in the middle of play—and all must be executed with equal power and precision.

Circle Turn: Oftentimes you hear coaches say that one of their players took the "tourist route" on a play and let his check score an easy goal. By "tourist route," the coaches mean that a player went for that long, leisurely, aimless glide through his turn around the net instead of making an abrupt switch of direction without any noticeable loss in stride. Coasting around the net can be, and usually is, fatal during a game. Turning the net in a clockwise direction understandably is considerably more difficult than turning in a counterclockwise direction, mainly because my preferred, power foot—the right one—is the "inside" foot on the left-to-right turn. In turning the net, I always create power and drive by pushing hard off my "outside" foot; consequently, it is

When skating around the net with or without a rival player in pursuit, the trick is to make the tightest turn possible and avoid the long tourist routes to the corners. I create power and speed by pushing hard off my outside foot, and I tilt my body to the inside—placing most of my weight on the inside blade, the one closer to the net.

easier for me and for most players to generate swifter speed on the counterclockwise turn than the clockwise turn, since my right foot then is the "outside" foot. During a game we probably make an equal number of counterclockwise and clockwise turns around the net, however, so we practice both of them during our workouts. Right to left or left to right, the skating technique is the same. As I start into the turn around the net, I tilt my body to the inside, placing most of my weight on the inside blade. Rather than drift around the net, though, I pull my outside leg—right or left, depending on the direction I am moving—around and over my inside leg; plant that outside leg hard onto the ice; and then push as hard as possible off the inside edge of the skate blade of that outside leg. Complicated? Not really, once you try it. The basic idea is to generate tremendous speed and power by using the outside leg as the driving force. Once I complete a turn around the net, I am always in full flight. My speed and momentum and power are there; I don't have to start all over again. Naturally, the toughest part of a turn around the net is the problem of controlling your outside foot. Don't let it float around in midair. Control it. Pump away with shorter strides, using strong leg drive. Also, try to keep the arc of the curve you make on a turn around the net as small as possible. If, for example, I start a turn around the net from twenty-five feet away down the so-called red icing line, I certainly do not go twenty-five feet down the same line on the other side of the net before starting up the ice. Turn the net as quickly as possible. At times my turns are so tight that I almost trip over the back of the goal; in fact, I have fallen over the netting. No matter; I definitely don't want to end up in the corner someplace. That's a waste of time and motion, and may cost my team a goal.

Crossover Turn: This is the most difficult skating maneuver a defenseman must perform during a game, since he must do it while skating backward. Let me create a situation. I'm skating backward down the ice as the opposition has a three-on-two break. Once across the blue line, the center fires the puck into the corner to my right, hoping that his left wing will beat me to the puck and center it back out in front of the net. My problem is that the left wing has a definite advantage over me because he is skating forward while I am moving in reverse. If I don't make a quick crossover turn without any loss in skating speed, he no doubt will beat me to the puck easily. To turn right, I instinctively move my right foot out slightly, then simultaneously push off that right foot and cross my left foot over the right, planting it head-on in the direction of the puck. Then I push off the inside of that left foot, bring the right foot back around and inside the left—and I'm in full flight. Balance is terribly important when I make this turn, so at the start of the crossover—just when I turn my foot in the direction I plan to go—I also consciously revolve my shoulders toward the position of the puck and have them lead my legs.

The crossover turn while skating backward is a time-saver for all defensemen. At the top, I have moved my right foot out slightly and pointed the skate in the direction I plan to go. In the lower picture, I already have swung my left foot over the right and now I'm pushing hard toward the puck.

Here I'm making a tight turn in front of the Boston net to chase after a rebound. My body leans in the direction I want to go— to the right in this picture—and I pivot off the outside edge of the blade on my inside skate.

Tight Turn: This is the turn forwards normally make when they are forechecking the opposition and defensemen employ while covering in front of their net. For instance, if Gregg Sheppard is checking his rival center and suddenly that player passes the puck to a teammate, Gregg cannot afford to stop quickly, turn around, and start up all over again—and he definitely can't think about taking the "tourist route" back up-ice by making a wide circle. On defense, if the goaltender has made a save but left a rebound in the area behind me, I have to make the quickest possible tight turn to get the puck out of danger. In making a tight turn, I lean my body in the direction I will go, pivot off the outside edge of the blade on my inside skate, bring my outside foot around, and then plant it ahead of that inside foot. Say I must make a tight turn to my right. I simply lean my body to the right, pivot on the outside edge of my right skate, pull my left foot around, and set it down ahead of my right foot—and then I'm away. I control the tightness of the turn with that pivot; the tighter I want to turn, the shorter I make the arc of my pivot.

Stopping

There are a number of different ways to brake yourself on the ice; in fact, during a normal game I use any number of stopping techniques. When coming to a stop, though, I always want to leave myself in perfect position for a sudden departure in some other direction. When I must stop myself while skating forward, I prefer to use the so called two-skate stop, which simply means I use both skates to brake my movement. Although I must be able to stop with either my right leg or my left in the lead—working as a brake—I once again prefer to lead with my right foot since it is my power foot. To stop, I simultaneously (1) turn my body slightly to the left or the right; (2) lean my body slightly to the back; (3) turn my skates in the same direction I turned my body; and (4) dig the blades of my skates into the ice with a cutting angle that creates flying ice chips. After stopping, I depart again by pushing off the foot that leads to whichever direction I want to go and then lifting my back foot over that lead foot. Oftentimes during a game I have to stop on one skate because of an unexpected play; when that happens, I make the same body and skate movements, brake with the inside edge of the lead skate, and then depart by using that same foot to push me away. At times I have to stop on just my rear foot, but I try to keep such brakings to a minimum. Why? Try it. As you'll discover, it's very easy to lose your balance when you stop on your back foot—and without good balance you will not be able to get a good start after you stop. Being a defenseman, I also make dozens of stops every game while skating backward. Oddly enough, such stops are not that difficult. What I do here is either make a "V" with my skates, cutting the inside edges of the blades into the ice, or stop the same way I do when skating forward.

At the end of the book, in the chapter devoted to conditioning, I list a number of excellent practice drills that will improve *your* skating if you work at it diligently.

In making a two-skate stop I turn my body, bend my knees to absorb the force, and dig the blades of both skates into the ice with a sharp cutting angle. This position provides maximum balance for the eventual takeoff in another direction.

CHAPTER THREE

Stickwork

Someone once told me that Arnold Palmer has five thousand golf clubs locked in a storeroom adjacent to his residence in Latrobe, Pennsylvania, and that when he thinks his driver or five iron or putter or any other club does not feel just right in his hands he immediately replaces it with a club selected from the storeroom vault. I also understand that in the same room Palmer has a complete set of machines and tools which he uses to reshape all his clubs—the grips, the shafts, the faces—to his personal specifications. Believe me, I don't have five thousand hockey sticks, or for that matter, even two hockey sticks, stacked in the guest bedroom of my apartment, and I don't have any hammers or drills in the kitchen, but I certainly understand why Palmer goes to such pain in an attempt to find golf clubs that feel right to him. Like golfers, hockey players also use a club to get their job done. We call it a hockey stick. And like Arnold Palmer with his golf clubs, I treat my hockey sticks with tender loving care. I test all my sticks before a game to determine if they have the exact feel I want. Sticks may weigh the same and look the same but still not feel the same. What determines whether or not a stick feels right when I pick it up? I really don't know. Something goes off in my head and tells me a certain stick feels super— or tells me to throw the stick back on the rack. If a stick doesn't feel "super" in my hands, I certainly won't use it in a game.

Think of all the things I do with my hockey stick. I use it to keep my balance at times. I stickhandle with it. I pass the puck with it. I take passes with it. I shoot the puck with it. I break up plays with it. Or put it this way: except for skating, everything I do on the ice, I do with my hockey stick. It is the second most important tool of my occupation. That's why I am so choosy about hockey sticks.

Stick Selection

This is another particular area where standard rules do not necessarily apply to professional hockey players. Why should we be so different? We play the game every day, of course, and over the years we have developed certain individual preferences that vary slightly from the norm. For instance, according to the traditional theory used to determine the correct length of a player's hockey stick, I should play with a stick that touches my chin when it is propped on the tip of its blade and set between my skates. If I happen to be wearing normal street shoes, the stick should touch my nose when held in the same position. However, the sticks I always use reach only the top of my shoulders when I am on skates and about my lower lip when I am in street shoes. It's strictly a question of feel as far as I am concerned. Ken Hodge of the Bruins stands about six feet three inches, compared to my five feet eleven inches, but our sticks are roughly the same length. His hands and mine reach practically the same point when we drop them straight down our sides. On the other hand, I could never use Yvan Cournoyer's sticks or Mike Walton's sticks; in fact, their sticks are so short—I doubt they even reach the middle of their chests—that ten-year-old kids probably would have trouble playing with them. However, Cournoyer and Walton both do all right with them, as their records prove.

Stick manufacturers claim that I am a "tough order," since I play with light sticks that have stiff shafts. Normally light sticks have whippy shafts and heavy sticks have stiff shafts; I prefer the combination of light and stiff. I always use a stick that weighs slightly less than one and one-half pounds. Before each game I take several of my specially made light sticks and test them for proper stiffness. If I create too much of an obvious bend in the shaft when I apply pressure from the top, then that stick is too whippy for me. If the shaft doesn't "give" too much, then I may use that stick in a game.

I carry my stick a little lower than the average player and also prefer to keep the blade and the puck well in front of me while skating, so I use sticks that rest between a Number 5 and a Number 6 lie. The lie of a stick is the angle between the blade and the shaft that determines whether the stick is flat or upright—or in between. The lower the lie, the wider the angle between the shaft and the blade; the higher the lie, the narrower the angle between the shaft and the blade. As that angle narrows, of course, sticks turn from flat to upright. All the Bruins use sticks with lies between Number 5 and Number 7, except for the goaltenders, whose sticks range between Number 10 and Number 13. Your skating style determines the lie of your stick. Esposito, for instance, is tall and skates more upright than most—so he uses a higher lie. His stick also feels about twice as heavy as mine—like a war club. On the other hand, Gregg Sheppard keeps the puck well away from his skates when he stickhandles, so he uses a stick with about a Number 5 lie. There is no definitive rule for determining the lie of *your* stick. What I recommend is that you put on your skates, go out onto the ice with a batch of sticks that have different lies, and test all of them for personal comfort and feel. Never test sticks for proper lie while you are standing barefoot or in your street shoes; after all, you play hockey wearing ice skates that make you several inches taller than you actually are. Two testing hints: (1) if a certain lie forces you to raise or lower your hands from the position you prefer to carry them on the ice, then that lie is not for you; (2) the blade of the stick must rest squarely on the ice when you hold it in your normal position, otherwise that particular lie is not made for you. Too many parents, I'm afraid, like to surprise their young hockey players by purchasing new sticks for them, but they don't know what lie to buy for them. As a result I always see little kids trying to shoot pucks with sticks that are bigger than they are and with sticks that rest on the ice only at the heel or the toe of the blades. It does not cost any more to get the *right* stick. And you will be able to handle the puck better with that *right* stick.

Most young hockey players don't realize it, but sticks also come in different blade lengths and widths. According to the official rules, the length of a blade from heel to toe cannot exceed twelve and one-half inches, while the width from bottom to top cannot be less than two inches or more than three inches. I use a ten-and-one-half-inch blade with a two-and-one-half-inch width. With that shorter and narrower blade I feel I can control the puck better while passing and stickhandling, and I can shoot with more authority because there is less room for the puck to stray on the blade. I honestly can feel the puck there on the blade. Control. That's the key word in determining the proper size of your hockey stick. If you continually lose the puck on your stick-handling maneuvers and seem to be getting off ineffective shots, then try another stick that perhaps you will handle better. It will help, I'm sure.

One of the worst things that ever happened to hockey was the curved-stick craze that hit the scene back in the mid-1960s. Now don't get me wrong. If Bobby Hull wants to use a hockey stick that looks like a boomerang, OK. If Stan Mikita and Phil Esposito and Rod Gilbert want to use sharply curved blades, OK. They play the game every day, and for the most part they have mastered the intricacies of the curved stick. However, a curved blade is basically a liability for young hockey players because it focuses their attention on shooting at the expense of such other maneuvers as passing and stickhandling. Worse than that, most young players—and, in fact, many players in the NHL—cannot control their shots with a curved stick and just fire away aimlessly at the net, hoping that the puck will dip or float past a surprised goaltender.

A curved stick almost totally eliminates the backhand shot from a shooter's arsenal. When the curved-stick craze was at its peak, I noticed that a number of NHL players happened to be in goal-scoring slumps; their best shots used to land in Section B, Row 3, Seat 9 of the mezzanine. Then the NHL wisely legislated against the excessive curves, ruling that the curvature of the blade could not exceed one-half inch. Now any player caught using an illegal stick gets a two-minute penalty on the spot and a hundred-dollar fine, so it's hardly worth the effort to cheat. Not coincidentally, I'm sure, some NHL players suddenly became great goal-scorers once the curvature was regulated; for instance, Vic Hadfield, then with the New York Rangers, immediately doubled his previous season's goal total and finished with fifty goals, a team record.

My own blade is curved slightly, perhaps about one-quarter of an inch down near the toe of the blade, but not only for shooting purposes. As a defenseman I must do a lot of stick checking, and I'm always trying to get the puck out of a corner. By using a stick with a slight curve at the toe, I can control the puck much better—and it is imperative that defensemen control the puck well. As you might guess, I don't recommend curved sticks for young players until they reach the point where they can "control" that type of stick, certainly not until they are at least in their teens. And if you happen to play center, you should *never, never, never* use a curved stick—simply because of the demands of your position. Centers must pass to their left and to their right; if a center happens to be a left-hand shot and uses a stick with a big curve, he no doubt will be unable to control backhand passes to his left wing. Also, centers oftentimes take pass-outs on their backhand side while standing in the slot and must dispose of the puck quickly in order to beat the goaltender; they simply do not have time to switch the puck onto their forehand side. Indeed, the backhand shot should be one of a center's best weapons. Jean Beliveau of the Canadiens scored more than five hundred goals during his great NHL career, and he estimates that about a hundred and fifty of those goals were scored on backhanders. Beliveau always used a straight blade on his stick.

Stick Preparation

There are approximately three hundred and sixty players in the National Hockey League, and I think I can safely say that very few of those three hundred and sixty players have ever read the league's official rule book from cover to cover. So there I was one October night in 1972, traveling with the Bruins on another airplane to another game in another city and browsing through the rule book. Actually, someone had given me a copy of the book, the regular friendly card game was over, the other guys were dozing, and there was nothing else to do. As I read through Section Three (Equipment—Sticks), Rule 20, Paragraphs (a), (b), (c), and (d), I thought to myself that one rule seemed to be missing. So I read Rule 20 again, and it still was not there. Then I checked through the rest of the book to see if it was part of some other rule. Still no mention of it. And that's how I became the first player in the NHL to play without tape wrapped around any part of the blade of his hockey stick.

Like every other player in the league, I had thought the rules stipulated that we had to put tape on the blades of our sticks, so I covered less than one and one-half inches of my ten and one-half inch blade with a sliver of black tape. When I discovered there was no such rule in the book, I asked some NHL authorities to clarify the taping situation. Later I was told that taping the blade was an option open to the individual player; if he didn't want to tape the blade, there was no rule against it. Great. No tape on the blade for me. In the old days players no doubt used tape to hold their blades together. Nowadays the blades of hockey sticks are precoated with fiber glass or some other adhesive to prevent them from splintering, so there is no need for tape on the blade.

For me the whole matter of tape on the blade once again comes down to the subject of "feel." Give me two identical sticks— one with a sliver of tape on the blade, the other without any tape—and I think I could tell you which stick doesn't have the tape. As far as I am concerned, tape adds unnecessary weight to my stick. Once I stopped taping the blades of my sticks, I noticed that a lot of other players stopped taping their sticks, too. One hockey writer even kept count of the number of players that switched to tapeless blades, and by the middle of the 1973–74 season the total had passed one hundred. On the other hand, Phil Esposito and Yvan Cournoyer, the two best pure goal-scorers in the NHL, not only tape the blades of their sticks, they tape them from heel to toe. Phil and Yvan obviously still hold to the old theory that a black puck snuggled against black tape on the blade of a stick may confuse a goaltender momentarily and cause him to lose sight of the puck in the black-in-black background. Considering their goal-scoring statistics, I am not about to disagree with them. However, I prefer the lighter feel I get from a stick without tape on the blade.

Believe it or not, I also scored a goal the very first time I touched a puck with a tapeless stick. We were playing against the Islanders in New York, and I had just returned to the Bruins' lineup after missing three weeks of the early season schedule with some lingering knee problems. Midway through the first period of that game we had a face-off to the right of the Islanders' goalie, and Tom Johnson, our coach at the time, sent me out for my first shift. I positioned myself in the middle of the ice, about ten feet inside the blue line, and, sure enough, Phil Esposito won the face-off and slid the puck back to me. It was sliding smoothly—perfect for a slap shot, so I drew back my stick, slapped at the puck—and then watched it fly through a maze of players and over the goaltender's shoulder. Luck.

I don't like to make suggestions to goaltenders, since I have never played in goal and definitely have no plans to play there. I do think, though, that goaltenders should wrap the blades of their big sticks with clean white tape. Why? The puck is black, of course, and oftentimes it rolls aimlessly around the goal mouth with the goaltender desperately trying to stick it away. If he has white tape on the blade of his stick, the goaltender should have an easier time distinguishing between the puck and the blade as he swipes at the disk.

Although I do not use tape on the blade of my stick, I do wrap three layers of white tape around the top of the shaft where I hold the stick with my right hand. Why? Two reasons: control and feel. Oftentimes during a game I lose control of my stick and then have to pick it up off the ice. Ever try picking up a plain hockey stick off the ice with your hockey gloves? It's a very tricky business because the protruding tips of the glove fingers hit the ice in such a way that it becomes impossible to wrap your fingers around the handle. The only solution to that problem is to remove one of your gloves and snatch the stick from the ice. Also, it is very easy to lose control of your stick while shooting the puck and doing various checking maneuvers because the handles of hockey sticks tend to be very slippery, as do the palms of hockey gloves. Most players solve both of these dilemmas by either putting a premolded rubberized knob or wrapping a whole roll of tape around the top part of the handle; that way, if they happen to drop their stick onto the ice, the knob will slightly prop up the handle and make it easier to grasp, or if the stick starts to slide from their grip while shooting or checking, they will possibly be able to check the slide when their top hand bumps against the knob. However, I do not use a knob at the end of my stick because I think it's too bulky and gets in the way too much. What I do is wrap three layers of tape around the handle so that the fingers and the palm of my top (right) hand make contact with tape and not wood. By doing this I develop a better feel—there's that word again—for the stick and the puck, and I also find the stick easier to handle. Even that thin layer props the stick enough that I can easily pick it off the ice, and the tape arrests any sliding of the stick in my hand. Caution: I know of some players who stopped using tape at the top of their sticks and switched to a tacky compound for a better grip only to find that the stick stuck to their glove. Tape does the job well enough.

In many ways I guess I'm pretty much like an Arnold Palmer

in that I refuse to play *my* game unless the so-called tool in my hands feels just right. Before each game I take about a dozen sticks from my rack; test them for the proper weight, stiffness, and size I want; select about five or six; then tape their handles and leave them alongside the other "game sticks" in the dressing room. Would you believe it? Four or five hours later, just as we are ready to go onto the ice for our warm-up, I'll pick up those same sticks that felt so super and suddenly a couple of them will feel like hammers or pencils in my hands. Then I run around the room searching for some new sticks. As I said, it's all in my head.

Holding the Stick

Rule Number One: Always hold the stick with both hands, regardless of your position on the ice. In every game I see players spoil good goal-scoring opportunities for their team by mishandling a sudden pass becaue they happen to have only one hand—usually the top one—on their stick at the time. I don't care who you are: you cannot control a hard pass, or even a soft pass, or take an effective shot at the goaltender if you have only one hand on the stick. Like all players, I keep the position of my top hand very constant and vary the position of my lower hand according to what I'm trying to do with the stick. The top hand gives "control" while the bottom hand provides "power."

My top hand, of course, is my right hand. I *grab* the top of the stick with that right hand and sort of shake hands with it. By that I mean I hold the handle tightly and wrap my palm and fingers around it firmly, thereby acquiring a solid grip. There is no loose space between my hand and the handle of the stick. In golf the players always talk about the direction in which the "V" between their thumb and index finger points when they hold the club. As I look down the shaft of the stick I see a "U" more than a "V"—and it runs straight up and down the shaft, not off in some cockeyed direction. In holding the stick with that top hand, I don't overlap my thumb onto the knuckles of any fingers. I want the firmest grip possible, so I keep my fingers tightly together and set my thumb naturally alongside my index finger. If some player tries to yank the stick from my top hand, he won't get it without a good tug-of-war first.

There are three basic positions for my bottom hand on the stick, depending, of course, on what I want to do with the puck: stickhandle with it, pass it, or shoot it. When stickhandling, I want maximum feel for the puck on the blade of the stick, so I keep my hands relatively close together at the top; in fact, they are about a glove's width apart. When passing the puck, I want a combination of good feel and good power, so I drop my bottom hand a bit lower on the handle so that the separation between my hands amounts to about a glove and one-half. When shooting

the puck, I want absolute maximum power and strength at the expense of everything else, so I drop my bottom hand as low as comfortably possible on the shaft. The lower that bottom hand, the lower my body will be to the ice; consequently I will get more *body* into the shot. My grip for the bottom hand is the same as my top hand—no loose spaces to be seen—except when I shoot a wrist shot. For a wrist shot I place my thumb so that it overlaps my index finger, and when I shoot the puck that thumb flies off the index finger and stays in midair somewhere. Why do I overlap the thumb? Feel. I simply find it easier to snap and roll my wrist when the thumb is on top of the index finger. More about that later.

The position of my left hand on the handle of the stick varies according to what I am doing with the puck. While stickhandling (far left), I keep the left hand relatively close to the right for maximum feel and comfort. While passing (left), I want a combination of feel and power, so I drop the bottom hand a little lower on the handle. While shooting slap shots (bottom), I want maximum power, so I move my left hand as far down on the shaft as I can.

Stickhandling is a lost art, mostly because players try to stickhandle too much. I don't bounce the puck back and forth on the blade of the stick. Instead, I sweep the puck from side to side with a controlled movement (above) or simply keep pushing it forward with the blade (right).

Stickhandling

The word is *stickhandling*. Not *dribbling*. You stickhandle with the puck and you dribble with the basketball. Trouble is, most kids stickhandle too much. They get the puck on their stick; slap it back and forth a few dozen times with heavy, ice-shattering chops of their stick; wait for the cheers from the crowd; then lose the puck to a pesky checker on the other team. What did they accomplish? Nothing. One of the general weaknesses of the players who skate for the Montreal Canadiens is that they are not particularly great stickhandlers. In fact, the Canadiens don't want their players to stickhandle with the puck; they insist that their players pass the puck. Now! Montreal plays what we call a "headmanning" style of hockey; the player with

the puck is under instructions to pass it forward to another
Canadien the instant he touches it. Or as Jean Beliveau once
explained: "the less you hang onto the puck, the less chance you
will lose it." I remember we were discussing stickhandlers once,
and someone mentioned that Montreal had only two or three
players who were good stickhandlers—Beliveau, Peter Mahovlich, and probably Henri Richard, all of whom happened to be
centers. "Yeah," I said jokingly, "all their other good stickhandlers were either traded or sent to Nova Scotia because they
couldn't pass the puck."

As a rushing defenseman, I do stickhandle with the puck a lot.
To me, stickhandling should not imply a repetitive thwack of

puck meeting blade, creating the sound drummers make when they are tired. Rather than bang the puck from side to side on my stick, I control it with easy back-and-forth sweeps of my blade or simply just sweep the puck forward by pushing it in front of the blade. While sweeping, I keep the puck well ahead of me so that I can see the puck, my teammates, and any rival checkers at the same time. For some reason kids like to keep the puck too close to their feet when they carry it; as a result, they occasionally must look down to see the puck and simultaneously lose all sight of their teammates and rival checkers. That's bad. Always keep the puck out away from your skates—practically at stick's length from your body. While stickhandling, you must always keep your head up, or else you no doubt will suddenly find yourself flat on the ice from a bodycheck.

One thing that really impressed me about the Soviet National Hockey Team in its series with Team Canada was the extraordinary stickhandling ability of the Russian players. They always handled the puck as though it was tied to their sticks, yet they never looked down at the ice. In fact, they considered their stickhandling so important that they practiced it during the pregame warmups. On a signal from Captain Boris Mikhailov, all the Soviet players took a puck and skated full speed around the zone inside the blue line for maybe two minutes. The twenty players moved among one another at almost breakneck speed, yet they never seemed to lose control of the puck. Of course, when a player loses the puck, he has to look down at the ice to find it again—and that always causes a major collision. Nyet. Nyet.

Passing

The first rule of passing the puck is *always* look where you are passing it. Even scrubbed-faced rookies know that, or at least they should. It was my second or third game as a professional, and the Bruins were playing the New York Rangers at the old Madison Square Garden. There I was, a rookie playing in the so-called Big City for the first time and naturally wanting to make a good impression. Early in the game I started up the ice with the puck, trailed, I thought, by two of my Boston teammates. As I crossed the New York blue line I heard one of those teammates cry "Bobby, Bobby," so I dutifully dropped the puck back to him and continued skating forward in order to screen his shot from the goaltender. The shot never came. The player who had cried "Bobby, Bobby" was Vic Hadfield of the Rangers, and when I finally turned around to see what had happened to the puck Hadfield not only had it on his stick, he was about to score against *my* goaltender. NEW YORK GOAL BY NUMBER 11 HADFIELD, ASSIST TO NUMBER 4 ORR. As I skated back to the Boston bench my head was down around my ankle, and I wondered what time the Parry Sound local pulled out of New York that night.

The Canadiens have practically patented the headman pass, but here Carol Vadnais is giving them some of their own medicine as he headmans the puck to a Bruin teammate who has skated between and beyond two Montreal players.

Always look where you plan to pass the puck, and always keep the puck near the middle of the blade.

How important is passing? So important that it is an art—not a job. There are approximately four thousand goals scored each season in the NHL, and passes lead directly to 99.44 percent of them. Good, crisp passes from teammates, as well as errant passes by the opposition. I know it is no coincidence that the teams with the best passing games generally are the teams that have been together the longest. And not coincidentally, those same teams usually finish in first place or win the Stanley Cup. For instance, the Canadiens always have one of hockey's best passing teams, if not the best; one reason, I'm sure, is that they rarely have more than three or four rookies on their roster who see regular action. Take the Bruins, too. In 1967 Harry Sinden

After releasing my pass I sweep my stick toward the target and keep it as low to the ice as possible.

put together three solid lines and two regular defense pairings, then told everyone to get acquainted. One line had Phil Esposito centering for Ken Hodge and Ron Murphy; another had Fred Stanfield centering for Johnny Bucyk and Johnny McKenzie; and the third had rookie Derek Sanderson centering for Ed Westfall and Eddie Shack. On defense Don Awrey teamed with Teddy Green, while I worked with Dallas Smith. Over the next five seasons the Bruins finished first twice, tied for first another time, and won two Stanley Cups. And over those five seasons we made only three real lineup changes: Wayne Cashman replaced the retired Murphy with Hodge and Esposito; Mike Walton, Wayne Carleton, and Don Marcotte became regular left wings at different times on the line with Sanderson and Westfall; and both Rick Smith and Carol Vadnais filled in on occasion for Teddy Green at defense. It's easier to win games and championships when you are well acquainted with the players on your team, as our record over those years proved conclusively.

What Sinden did with the Bruins back in 1967 also should serve as a good lesson for many of the inexperienced hockey men who volunteer to coach kids' teams. Too many coaches constantly shuffle their lines during practices and games, almost poking in the dark for the right line combinations. They never give their players a chance to develop the on-ice rapport that a line needs to be effective. Listen. It took time for even an Esposito to learn when, where, and how Hodge wants the puck—and vice versa. I have played alongside Dallas Smith for most of the last seven years, and while we have established sort of a mental telepathy between us on the ice, there are times we confound one another by doing something totally new and totally un-

expected. So how can coaches expect their nine-year-old right wing to figure out that his eight-year-old linemate will fake left at the red line, go right, turn back in, burst forward, cut outside, and then look for a pass off the sideboards—if the youngsters never have been on the ice together before? It takes time.

During any game I regularly make four types of passes to my teammates. Or at least I hope they always go to my teammates. In making *forehand* and *backhand* passes I try to slide the puck to another Bruin with a low, sweeping motion, almost like I'm sweeping a floor. The trick in making forehand and backhand passes is to keep the puck flat on the ice at all times. To do this, I barely lift my stick off the ice, if I remove it at all, and I try to keep the puck in the middle of the blade throughout the sweeping motion. If I raise the blade of my stick, of course, the puck will fly into the air, and that's the last thing I want to happen. On my follow-through, I sweep my stick toward the target, which helps keep the puck on my intended line. The *drop* pass poses more

Andre Savard of the Bruins is one of hockey's best young playmaking centers. Here he spots linemate Don Marcotte skating behind Bill Fairbairn of the Rangers and hits him with a long, low flip pass that Fairbairn cannot intercept.

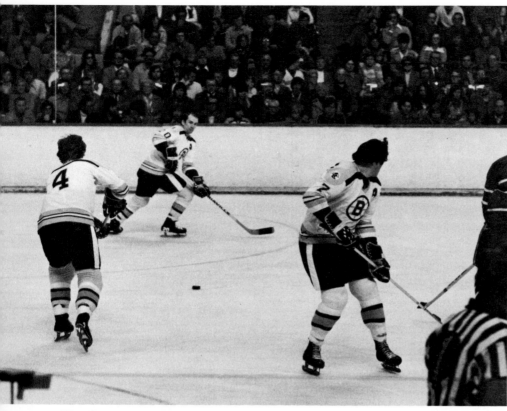

The Canadiens cut off the passing and skating lanes to my right, so I turn the other way and pass the puck to Dallas Smith, who has plenty of skating room. Notice how Dallas gave me a perfect target by keeping the blade of his stick on the ice and extending it well forward. If possible, my pass should never leave the ice.

difficult problems, aside from the problem of possibly dropping the puck to the wrong man as I did that night in New York when I passed to Hadfield for a Ranger goal. With the Bruins we employ the drop pass mainly in two ways: (1) coming out of our zone, the puck carrier drops the puck to the trailer when or if he feels that he cannot avoid the forechecking forwards; (2) breaking into the opponents' zone on a two-on-one or a three-on-two, the puck carrier leading the play drops the puck to the trailer and then tries to screen the trailer's shot at the goaltender. Once the lead puck carrier drops the puck, he almost certainly will get bodychecked by some player on the other team. That's the physical risk involved with the drop pass. In dropping the puck to a teammate, I want to make certain that it rests dead and flat on the ice for him. If I leave the puck rolling or spinning, my teammate most likely will be unable to fire a good, quick shot at the goaltender. To drop the puck that way, I stickhandle to the spot where I want to leave the puck. Once there I stop the forward movement of the puck by letting it come to rest against the back side of my blade. Then I continue forward, forgetting about the puck but keeping the blade of my stick on the ice to hide the puck from the goaltender.

Finally, there is the *flip* pass, easily the most difficult pass to

execute. Here's an example of when and why I would use a flip pass: I have the puck and want to get it to a teammate fifteen feet away but a rival checker is close by and ready to intercept a normal forehand or backhand pass along the ice. The only solution is the little flip pass over the checker's stick. Trouble is, flip passes are extremely difficult to control because they do leave the ice. In flipping a pass I get the puck as close to the toe of my blade as possible and then simply flick my wrists. The puck will pop into the air. Controlling the flip pass is strictly a matter of feel and luck. The perfect flip pass will pop over the checker's stick, return immediately to the ice, and then slide smoothly to my teammates. Unfortunately that happens maybe once every ten tries. Because of the element of luck involved with flip passes, I practice them more than other passes. At every workout I get another Bruin, and for three or four minutes we flip a puck back and forth. If I get the puck to land flat within a couple of inches of my intended target, I'm extremely happy, believe me.

One pass I have excluded from this discussion is the *slap* pass. I forgot about the slap pass a long time ago, and you should forget about it, too. There is no way you can control a pass when you slap at the puck. So forget it.

Two reminders: when passing, always lead the receiver so that he won't have to break his skating stride to handle the puck; and *never* pass the puck across the front of your own net. I like to think of my potential receivers the same way I think of ducks when I'm out in a blind; that is, I want to *lead* them with the puck. I'd much rather overshoot a teammate by twenty feet with a pass then undershoot him by two inches. If a receiver has to stop or even slow down to take a pass, he may take a heavy body-check for his trouble. Then again, as someone once said, if you don't like a guy, why not put the pass in his skates? Only joking, of course.

Pass Receiving

There is no way a passer can judge precisely how much he should lead the receiver. As I said earlier, passing depends to a great extent on the particular rapport between the passer and the receiver. Receivers can help a passer by keeping their stick on the ice and letting it act as a target for the passer. When taking a pass, the receiver should loosen the grip on his stick slightly and try almost to cup the puck with the blade by laying it over the top of the puck. If a receiver holds his stick too firmly, the blade will not have any give or feel, and the puck will tend to bounce away. Not all passes are perfect; they oftentimes do end up in a player's skates.

When that happens I do one of two things, depending on the player traffic where I am on the ice. If there's no one near me, I turn the blade of one of my skates in such a way that the puck will slam against it and stop almost on the spot. Then I kick the puck forward, take it with my stick, and head away. However, if I am surrounded by a crowd of players, I turn one of the blades at an angle so that the puck will carom off the skate blade and slide away. Controlling the puck in your skates is not that difficult. Terry O'Reilly of the Bruins may not skate like a Cournoyer, but he is one of the best players in the NHL at handling the puck when it gets into his skates. After all our practices he stays on the ice, discards his stick, and then maneuvers a puck with his skates for ten minutes. So, really, don't give up on a pass just because it does not arrive on the middle of your stick.

Skate blades can be as important as your stick for receiving passes. Here I stop the puck with the blade of my right skate and will kick it forward with my left skate.

CHAPTER FOUR
Shooting

It's funny how certain things always stick in your mind. On Friday afternoon, September 1, 1972, I sat about ten rows up from the blue line at the Montreal Forum and got my first live look at the players on the Soviet National Team as they worked out the day before the start of their series against Team Canada. Looking at them skate around the ice, I immediately thought they were two dozen Claude Provosts, because they all seemed to skate with short, choppy, bowlegged strides. Even so, they moved quickly and avoided the tourist routes. It was also obvious that they could pass the puck with speed and precision and knew how to handle it with both their sticks and skates. What I almost laughed at that day, though, was their shooting. The Russians were the original gang that couldn't shoot straight. They shot the puck off their wrong foot. Their weight was in the wrong place. Their shots had no zip or zing and always seemed to miss the net by wide margins. Clearly, the scouting reports we had been given on the Russians were 100 percent correct: they could do everything a hockey player had to do—except shoot.

But I learned the next night that the Russians had played possum for our benefit during that drill in the Forum. In Game 1 the Soviets unleashed some of the quickest, hardest, most accurate shots I had ever seen and went on to beat us 7 to 3. I remember one goal perfectly, since it came straight from the textbook on shooting. Valery Kharlamov, the swift Soviet right wing, picked up the puck in his own end, cruised neatly up the ice, faked right but turned left just inside our blue line and then, while still accelerating to his left, fired a bullet that zinged past goaltender Ken Dryden for what later proved to be the game-winning goal. Kharlamov's shot was everything a shot should be: he surprised the goaltender by shooting when he did; he got the puck away quickly; he fired the puck accurately to an unprotected corner of the net; and he put great force and power behind the shot. Now my only criticism of Russian shooters is that they don't shoot the puck often enough; if anything, they pass too much.

In every hockey game teams waste dozens of good scoring opportunities because players foolishly attempt *one* extra pass. If I have the puck twenty feet in front of the net and the goaltender has generously left me four large openings, I'm certainly not going to pass the puck to a teammate, no matter how uncovered he appears to be. Maybe my pass will hop over his stick or be intercepted by a backchecker. Possibly the goaltender's position that is so open for me is totally shut for him. When I have good position for a shot, I take it. Even if the goaltender stops the puck, he probably will leave a good rebound for one of my teammates near the net. Of course, when I don't have that good open shot I do try to pass the puck to a teammate.

There is no substitute for a shot at the goaltender

How important is shooting? Look at Phil Esposito, a gunner's gunner. In 1970–71 Phil took 550 shots at rival goaltenders, breaking Bobby Hull's previous NHL record by 136 shots. Phil also scored 76 goals that season to break Hull's previous record of 58 goals. When Esposito gets the puck in front of the net, he doesn't stop to ask questions or look around for someone to pass the puck to. Why should he? Phil has worked long and hard to develop the quickest "snap" shot hockey has ever seen, though goaltenders normally don't see his "snap" shot until it has flown past them. Even when the goaltenders are lucky enough to stop one of Phil's bullets, they are so staggered by its force that they are helpless to protect against a rebound shot. The same year Esposito scored those 76 goals, he also assisted on 76 other Boston goals. And I dare guess that 20 or 25 of those assists actually were rebounds of his original shots.

Or look at my own statistical record. Over a complete season I generally take twice as many shots on goal as any other defenseman in the league. Shots on goal are one of the three indicators I use to determine my effectiveness in a particular game. The others are the final score and the number of times I was on the ice when the opposition scored. Midway through the 1973–74 season I scored the two-hundredth goal of my seven-and-one-half-year NHL career, and at the same time I was closing in on 500 career assists. Of those 200 goals, I'd say that probably 100 came on shots from the vicinity of my right-point position, 60 came on shots from the ten-foot to thirty-five-foot range, 35 came on shots around the goal mouth, and 5 came on shots into an empty net during the closing seconds of play. In breaking down my assists, I'd guess that as many as 150 really were rebounds or deflections of my shots. So, as you can see, when you are in the attacking zone, there really is no substitute for a shot at the goaltender.

Believe me, though, you don't become a good shooter by accident. Esposito, for example, remains on the ice for fifteen or twenty minutes after almost all our workouts and practices his shooting techniques. He doesn't just drop down a dozen pucks and snap them at the goaltender; he practices the shots he makes most often in a game. To start, he gets someone—another Bruin player, one of the trainers, the coach, or even a popcorn vendor—to stand in the corner and repeatedly fire pucks into his skates as he stands in his normal position around the slot. Once the puck arrives in his feet, in one motion Phil tries to kick it onto his stick and shoot it on the goal. After that he calls for pass-outs directly onto his stick as he roams around the slot; again he tries to take the pass and snap the puck all in one strong, quick, fluid motion. Finally, Phil starts circling in front of the net and tries to deflect shots from the blue line. I'm sure fans think deflected goals are 99 percent luck. They are at least 60 percent skill.

Only practice makes a good shooter. When I was not skating out on the ice back in Parry Sound, I was down in the garage shooting thousands of pucks against the back wall. The ice there was a piece of smooth plywood, and the pucks were a couple of ounces heavier than regular pucks because my father had cut out the middles and filled them with lead. Practice and strength are necessary. The best shooters in the NHL all have strong and muscular forearms, wrists, and hands. The more you shoot, of course, the stronger your arms will become. Yvan Cournoyer's forearms make Rod Laver's look like needles. Dale Tallon of the Chicago Black Hawks has such strong wrist action that he can hit a golf ball longer than two hundred yards without taking more than a three-foot backswing. Rick Martin of the Buffalo Sabres, the best young shooter in the game, has unbelievably strong and large hands. He palms a basketball as though it was a Ping-Pong ball, and he probably could squeeze the air out of that basketball if someone thought to ask.

Besides shooting a puck on the ice or in a garage, there are some other basic ways to develop good muscle tone in your arms. I still lift weights a few days a week in the off season, not to see how much weight I can bench-press but to exercise the muscles I use most often while playing hockey. I also keep a set of dumbbells at my apartment and work with them for ten or fifteen minutes maybe every other day. My dumbbells weigh only about twenty pounds apiece. I don't want to become Mr. Universe, I simply want to strengthen the muscles I use most often and keep them in proper tone. When you watch television at night, why not get a couple of hard rubber balls and idly squeeze them for a half hour every evening during your favorite show? I guarantee that you will feel the difference in your hands, wrists, and forearms after only a couple of weeks.

One word of caution: don't substitute a rubber ball for the puck when practicing your shooting in the garage or anyplace else. A rubber ball weighs considerably less than a puck, sits differently on the ice and the ground and, because of its shape, tends to fly uncontrollably. When practicing at any sport, never use an object lighter than the object you use during official competition.

So let's shoot. All shots fall into four categories: *wrist, slap, flip* and *deflections*, each of which we will discuss very carefully. Backhand shots and the so-called snap shot that Phil Esposito learned from Bobby Hull when they were teammates in Chicago both are members of the wrist group. I would guess that 60 percent of my first 200 goals were scored on slap shots, 35 percent were scored on wrist shots, and the other 5 percent were scored on flip shots. The ratio between wrist and slap shots is always closer for a defenseman than a forward, since defensemen generally shoot more slap shots than forwards. We shoot from greater distances, of course, and I know that my slap shot reaches the goal much faster than my wrist shot. So while I may score more than half *my* goals on slap shots, forwards such as Esposito, Cournoyer, and Martin probably score less than 10 percent of *their* goals on slap shots.

Bearing in mind that percentage breakdown, which is fairly standard throughout hockey, I really don't understand why young kids usually practice only their slap shot, at the expense of the other shots. When I drive around Boston or other cities and see kids playing street hockey or skating on a municipal rink, I always find that they prefer the slap shot about nine to one over any other shot. In fact, they always seem to have the stick wrapped around their head, ready to slap it down against the puck. Even when they are fifteen feet from the goal. Ridiculous. In practicing your shooting, strive for the balanced program applicable to your particular position. If you are a center, work on your wrist shot twice as much, and with twice the intensity, as you practice your slap shot. If you are a defenseman, spend about equal time on both shots. The best slap shot in the world won't do you one bit of good if the checkers in the slot don't allow you time to get it away. What good is a slap shot when a two-foot flip shot over the goaltender's extended leg will do a quicker and better job?

Shooting Technique

I don't believe there are any "secrets" for becoming a better hockey player, except hard work and constant practice. However, after years of experimentation with hundreds of different shooting techniques, I have concluded that there is one "secret" for becoming a better shooter. Let me explain. The great, great majority of players in the NHL shoot basically the same way. In releasing the puck from the blade of their stick, they roll their wrists *over* and practically hood the blade. What this means is that the blade does not follow the puck toward the target; instead, the blade moves from the release point and circles around in front of the shooter's body. In golf language, they hook their shot. To my way of thinking, that is inefficient form.

I never roll my wrists over. I roll tham *under*. By doing that I keep the blade of my stick directly on line with the puck throughout the follow-through of my shot. In golf language, I guess I fade my shot. What I really do, though, is *control* the puck with a firmer, snappier wrist motion and then a targeted follow-through. To my way of thinking, that is the best form. I roll my wrists *under* on all my shots.

Wrist Shot

In recent years some of the better goal-scorers in hockey, like Esposito, Cournoyer, Bobby and Dennis Hull, have been calling their wrist shot a "snap" shot. Wrist or snap, they basically are the same shot because it is a triggerlike snap of the wrists that unleashes the shot at the poor goaltender. I am a left-handed shot, which means that my right hand holds the top of the stick and guides it while my left hand is down lower on the shaft and provides the power for the shot. For a wrist shot, I move that left hand well down onto the shaft until it reaches a comfortable position. The lower that left hand, the more power I will get into the shot. I hold the stick firmly, almost as though I'm trying to make sawdust out of the handle, and apply slightly more pressure with my bottom hand than my top. When I shoot a forehand wrist shot, the puck comes from my left as I look at the goal-tender. For a backhand wrist shot, the puck comes from my right as I look at the goaltender. Technically speaking, there is only one slight difference in the detailed execution of the two shots; for a backhand wrist shot I drop my bottom (left) hand even lower onto the shaft in an attempt to generate power. Let's stick with the forehand shot for now, since forehanders outnumber back-handers probably ten to one during a game.

As I get ready to shoot, I turn my body to the left so that I confront the puck head-on. In doing this, I set my back (left) foot ahead of the puck and point the toe of my right foot toward the target. Most players prefer to have the puck on either the toe or the heel of the blade of their stick when they fire their wrist shot. Not me. I want it directly in the middle of the blade for control. By keeping the puck in the middle, I build in margins for error toward both the heel and the toe; if the puck starts to roll either way from the middle of my blade during the shooting process, it still should be somewhere on the blade when I trigger the release. I have seen countless players who shoot their wrist shots from either the toe or the heel ruin tremendous scoring opportunities, because the puck rolled off their stick as they un-leashed their shot. Or as the radio and television announcers like to say: "He fanned on the puck." That's embarrassing, of course, and one simple way to avoid that type of embarrassment is to keep the puck in the middle of your blade while shooting wrist shots. Simple. Now I'm ready to shoot.

I start the puck from a position slightly behind my back (left) foot. The trick is to get my arms and stick as far back as possible without losing my balance, power, and firmness. As I bring the puck forward, my wrists are cocked; my head is over the puck as much as I can comfortably get it; and my weight is moving for-ward. Remember, when shooting never let your weight get to the rear; it should be moving forward at all times. Transferring the puck from behind my back foot to the release position up front is a delicate job. Some players jerk the puck to the front, others chop it, and still others gently pull it. I try to sweep the puck forward with a strong, fluid motion that permits me to maintain solid control over the disk at all times. Too many players, I'm afraid, let the puck control them during the execution of a wrist shot and eventually misfire or fan on the puck as they try to get their shot away.

I can release the puck at any point during my sweep simply by uncocking my wrists, rolling them under — not over, remember — and then following through on the shot. Barring on-ice compli-cations between the goaltender and myself, such as a defenseman who may be sliding toward me in an attempt to block my shot, I never release the puck from the blade of my stick until I reach the natural end of my sweep. I say "natural end" because the

I teach young hockey players to roll their wrists under with a firm, snappy motion when shooting the puck and then follow through with the blade extended toward the target.

end of each sweep will vary according to my particular stance, the distance between my feet and the puck, the contour of my body as it leans over the shot, and the position of my left (bottom) hand on the stick. Once I reach the natural end of my sweep, I'm ready to blast away at the goaltender.

Let's examine my physical position there at the end of my sweep: (1) my head is slightly behind the puck and the blade, with my eyes riveted directly at my target; (2) all my body weight has completed an orderly, balanced shift onto my right foot; and (3) my left (back) foot is dangling somewhere in outer space. Despite what a lot of instructors may say, forget about any so-called proper position for your back foot during the shot. Mine flies in a different direction just about every shot. Yvan Cournoyer wraps his left foot around his seat. Barry Wilkins of the Vancouver Canucks raises his back foot so high that he practically kicks himself in the ear. As I figure it, my back foot is about 99 percent weightless when I shoot the puck, so how can I ever expect to control it? If I start worrying about harnessing that back foot, I will lose some of the forward body force and momentum so necessary for an effective shot. One thing I will say

Even though it is less accurate, I always prefer to slap the puck when I am shooting from out near the blue line because the puck will reach the goaltender with greater speed and force. As you can see here, I had a good-sized opening to the goaltender's left side and managed to fire the puck past him.

about the back foot is that you shouldn't let it rise too high, certainly not above your waistline, or you will tend to lose your balance very easily.

In releasing the puck, I uncock my wrists with a quick snap—rolling them under, not over—and throw my hundred ninety-two and a half pounds behind the shot with full force. At that precise instant something strange happens. You might call it a "thumb-up." For wrist shots, I alter the grip of my bottom hand slightly and have the thumb overlap the index finger. Now, just as I snap-snap my wrists, that thumb flies off the index finger and sort of stays in an extended, upright position. Thumb up. Once all that has happened, and as the puck shoots toward its intended

target, I feel as though my front big toe is supporting my entire body. To get maximum power behind my shot, I must put every ounce into it, which means that all my weight must be in an absolute forward position. Believe me, I can't be more forward than to have all my weight perched there on the big toe of my right (lead) foot. Once in this one-legged position, I control the trajectory of my shot by letting the blade of the stick lead me into a natural follow-through. If I want to keep the puck low or even along the ice, I keep the blade of the stick low or even along the ice as I move into my follow-through. If I want to get the puck higher (the goal, remember, is four feet high and six feet wide), I lift the blade of the stick higher. High shot or low shot, I keep

For a slap shot, I keep my head almost directly over the puck and drop my bottom hand very low on the handle of the stick. I take the stick back low, with my arms fully extended, and I try not to get my hands much higher than my waist. At impact (right) my weight is forward, and I make contact directly behind the puck.

114

the blade of my stick dead on line with my target for as long as possible. As I continue through the natural completion of the shot, my hips turn open, squaring my body so that I am dead on the goaltender, and my back (left) leg returns to the ice almost alongside my right leg. This is a "must" ending for the follow-through since it leaves me in a balanced position from which I can easily skate off in any direction.

Slap Shot

Everyone loves the slap shot, mostly because it draws ooohs and aaahs from the fans. It is just that, too, a slap at the puck. Unlike a wrist shot, which I can control to a great extent, the slap shot is a luck shot. I probably will hit the net nine times out of ten with my wrist shot from the right point. However I probably will miss the same net at least five times out of ten with my slap shot. Another negative aspect of the slapper is that it takes considerably longer to get away than the wrist shot, thus increasing the possibility that either a backchecker or a shot-blocking defenseman will be able to interfere with the release and/or the flight of the shot. The slap shot must be used judiciously. For defensemen, though, the slap shot offers one distinct advantage as we stand there at the point and prepare to fire away at the net: I know that my weakest slap shot no doubt will reach the area of the net as fast as, if not faster than, my strongest wrist shot.

Basically my slap shot is a technical extension of my wrist shot, with only a few variants. In a wrist shot, I sweep the puck forward and then release it at the natural conclusion of my sweep. For a slap shot, the puck rests stationary on the ice; it is not attached to my stick and part of any sweeping movement. Of course, I want to slap the puck at the precise point where the blade of my stick connects with the ice. Or, as golfers like to say, I want the puck to be situated at the bottom of the swing. That is my natural point of impact and the place where I can slap the puck with full force. My best impact point seems to be slightly forward of the middle of my stance as I confront the puck, so that is where I try to position myself for a slap shot. And I try to get my head almost directly over the puck in order to establish better feel for what I want to do. To create more power and to get myself down closer to the puck, I drop my bottom (left) hand lower on the stick than it is for a wrist shot.

The trouble with most young hockey players who idolize the slap shot is that they think they must bring the stick back in a high, looping arc in order to create power for their shot. Some backswings really look comical. I remember one nine-year-old boy at my camp who always looked as though he was trying to write his name in the sky when he drew his stick back for a slap shot. Another youngster actually zonked himself on his helmet

with the blade of his stick. As a result of their long backswings, kids don't hit the puck smoothly at the impact point; instead, they chop at it, slice it, hook it, top it, and even miss it. They have no control whatsoever over the movement of their stick. I once saw a boy not only miss the puck but also miss the ice as he whipped his stick down from the heavens somewhere and tried to slap at the puck. We called him "Windmill" after that.

When I use the slap shot, I bring the stick back very low and never let my hands go above my waistline; consequently, the blade will not get too high above my waistline either. What I do is *control* my backswing. It may not draw the ooohs and the aaahs from the crowd, but control gets the job done much better. Once back, I start forward with the same basic technique that I use for a wrist shot. My weight moves forward in an orderly and balanced manner, and as I make contact directly behind the

The strobe photo on the left shows how my weight shifts to the forward foot during a slap shot. Balance comes from the extended back foot, as seen above during one of Phil Esposito's very rare slap shots.

puck all my weight is on my front foot and my back (left) foot is dangling again. As with the wrist shot, I regulate the height of my slap shot by keeping the blade of my stick low, high, or in between during the natural follow-through. And when I complete the shot my body has turned squarely toward the goaltender, my feet are set evenly apart, and I am ready to join the play without any problems.

Over the years I also have developed what I call a "quick slap shot." I will not use the regular slap shot unless I have adequate time to release it properly. My quick slap shot is just that: I get it away quickly. I need such a shot because of the frequent gambles I like to take at the blue line in an attempt to break up plays, intercept clearing shots, or just plain keep the puck in the zone. Example: We were playing the Rangers in what would turn out to be the final game of the 1972 Stanley Cup play-offs.

Eddie Giacomin of the Rangers won this one-on-one match-up against Ken Hodge of the Bruins. Hodge screened Giacomin (left), collected the loose rebound (center), and then tried to flip the puck over the goaltender's outstretched pad. No luck for Hodge this time.

Midway through the first period there was a scramble for the puck near the face-off circle to the left of Ranger goaltender Gilles Villemure. Suddenly the puck shot out toward me at the point, compliments of two of my teammates, Johnny Bucyk and Wayne Cashman, who had pried it loose from one of the New York defensemen. Two other Rangers were chasing the puck as it slid toward me. Clearly I did not have time to fire a regular slap shot or a wrist shot at the goaltender; in fact, I'm certain the two Rangers thought I'd simply shoot the puck back down the boards and into the corner. Time for my quick slap shot. All I want to do, really, is slap the puck as quickly as possible and get it moving toward the goaltender. Maybe it will catch him by surprise. Maybe it will be deflected en route and fly into the net. Maybe one of my teammates will get a rebound and put the puck into the net. In shooting my so-called quick slap shot I eliminate almost all body movement and bring the blade of the stick back less than, oh, eighteen inches. I don't worry about getting all my power into the shot. I just want to get the shot away as quickly as possible. As it turned out that night in New York, the puck shot through a maze of players and flew past Villemure, who was screened and never saw the shot. More importantly, we went on to win the game 3 to 0 and take the cup.

Flip Shot

Like all players, I use the flip shot primarily to get the puck up and over the goaltender when I am within about ten feet of the net. Johnny Bucyk of the Bruins has practically made a career of scoring goals on flip shots. The Chief likes to plant himself near the corner of the crease to the goaltender's right, particularly during our power plays. In that spot he is always ready for (1) a pass-out from the corner; (2) a pass across the goal mouth; or (3) a rebound of some other player's shot. Once the Chief gets the puck, he has the goaltender begging for mercy. Most times the goaltender is either stretched across the goal mouth or sliding across the crease with either his legs or his hands in the lead. Many players tend to panic in these situations and shoot the puck right into the sprawled goaltender. Not Bucyk. John, who uses one of the shortest sticks in the NHL in order to get maximum puck control, works the puck out onto the toe of his blade and calmly flicks it over the prone goaltender and into the net.

In shooting my flip shot, I also get the puck onto the toe end of the blade and then sort of scoop the puck into the air with a sharp snap-snap of my wrists, rolling them sharply under as I release the puck. The flip shot is not a power shot by any means. It is a finesse move during which I usually have an advantage

119

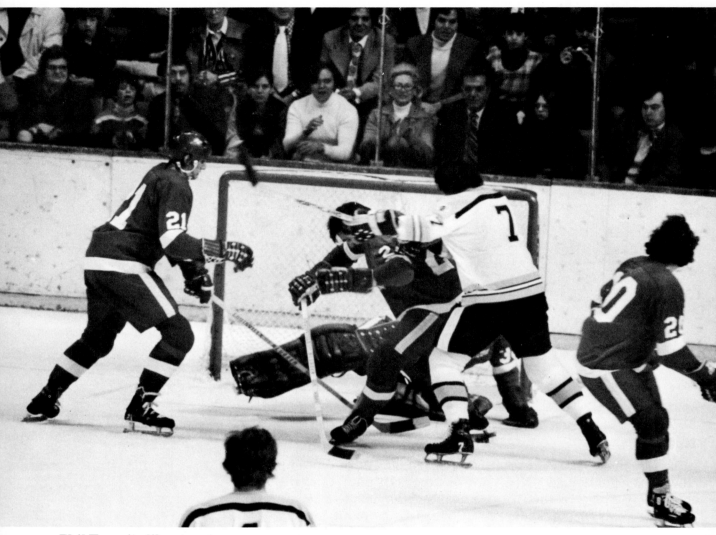

Phil Esposito likes to set up housekeeping in the slot in front of the net. Defensemen are paid to keep centers like Esposito out of the slot—so the resulting battles around the net get hot and heavy in every game.

over the goaltender because he is either down on the ice or in the process of going down, and most likely does not have great control over his movements. I remember a game against the Rangers in the 1970 Stanley Cup play-offs when I broke through two New York defensemen and suddenly found myself only six or eight feet from goaltender Eddie Giacomin. Giacomin split, flopping to the ice and spreading his legs to both sides. I moved slightly to my left, since it was the only way I could go and still retain control of the puck. My problem was this: Giacomin was spread out in such a position that his right leg pad, his stick, and his right arm combined to close off all but about six inches of the net. The top six inches, mind you. The trick was to scoop the puck up and over Giacomin's leg, stick, and arm and still get it into the net. As I remember, I gave the puck a double scoop, almost trying to pick it up, and then it barely flew over Giacomin and just caught the top of the net. If I had tried any other type of shot, Giacomin would have stopped the puck easily.

Deflections

As a defenseman I don't have the opportunity to deflect many shots toward the rival goaltender because one of the Bruins forwards usually deflects *my* shot at the goaltender. Ask any goaltender, and I'm certain he'll confess that deflections are the toughest kind of shot for him to stop. When the puck is coming toward him, the goaltender is moving to stop it. Suddenly some player tips the puck slightly, changing its course, and the goaltender is in trouble. Many times, too, defensemen accidentally deflect the puck past their own goaltender, which causes total embarrassment. I've deflected twelve or fifteen rival shots past my goaltenders in Boston, and I'm going to tip some more past them before I hang up my skates. Not purposely, of course, but oftentimes the puck gets lost in a melee of players and suddenly richochets off your stick and cruises past the goaltender. There's nothing you can do when that happens, except of course to try and get the goal back.

Some deflections come immediately to mind. One was in a game between New York and Chicago during the Stanley Cup play-offs a few years ago. It was the fifth game of the series, the teams were tied at two games apiece, and the score was tied fairly late in the game. Chicago Coach Billy Reay signaled for a line change while play continued, so a Black Hawk rookie named Bobby Schmautz — now a Bruin teammate — skated to the red line with the puck and fired it harmlessly into the far corner, or so he thought. Seeing Schmautz's clearing shot, goaltender Ed Giacomin reacted instinctively and followed by moving to his right. However, while the puck was in mid-flight to the corner, a Ranger defenseman foolishly swiped at it, hit it around his shoulders, and changed the direction of the puck. Eddie was helpless as the deflected puck flew to his left and caught the corner of his net. It was a ninety-foot goal. Chicago won the game on Schmautz's deflection and later won the series, too.

I clearly remember two other deflections that worked to my advantage in the same game early in the 1973–74 season when the Bruins were playing the Rangers at the Boston Garden. It seems that I'm always remembering incidents from games against New York, but our games with the Rangers have always been well played and, therefore, easy to remember. Early in the game I scored a goal on a backhand flip shot that bounced between a couple of players and eluded Giacomin. Later on I scored two more goals, getting the fourth hat trick of my career, and both of them were deflected behind Giacomin by his own defensemen. The first was a legitimate deflection by the Ranger defenseman, since he was caught in a swarm of players and simply was trying to block the shot. The second deflection, though, was definitely a bad play by Giacomin's defenseman.

As I fired away from the point, I had a clear line at Giacomin. Even so, there are not many players in any league, including the NHL, who will beat a goaltender from the point with any kind of shot if the goaltender has a perfect view of the puck right from the start. My shot was not very hard and probably was going to miss the right side of the net by a foot. Giacomin was prepared to handle it easily. While the puck was en route to Giacomin, though, a Ranger defenseman thrust the blade of his stick toward the puck, and tipped it over Giacomin's right shoulder. So instead of missing the goal by maybe a foot to Giacomin's left, the puck beat him on his right side. We happened to be winning the game by a big score at the time, and the deflection—on top of everything else that had happened to him—so irritated Giacomin that he threw his stick onto the ice and hurled his gloves into the air. I couldn't blame him.

If I played forward, I would certainly spend a few minutes each practice trying to deflect shots from various points inside the zone. The technique is fairly simple: hold the stick looser than you do when you are shooting the puck, then angle the blade of the stick toward the goaltender. As the shooter releases the puck, keep your eyes on it and calculate how much you should try to deflect it, and where. Better yet, the next time you attend an NHL game, study some of the better deflection specialists in the league: Esposito, Stan Mikita, Jean Ratelle, Bobby Clarke, Dave Keon, and watch how they position their bodies and their sticks to execute deflections. Watch them before the shot, not after it.

Practice all the principles of shooting. As you grow older, build your muscles and acquire more confidence in your ability to execute shots properly. You should also develop the various moves, shifts and "dekes" that distinguish the good shooters from the bad shooters. Don't make it easy for yourself, or else it will be harder for you in the end. For instance, I don't understand why coaches limit shooting practice to the so-called breakaway drill. How often do you get a breakaway in a game? Maybe there's one per team, but even that is a lot. Nevertheless, coaches seem to want to give their young players the psychological satisfaction of beating the goaltender and getting a chance to rehearse their stick-in-the-air salute. But that's the easy way out. At my camp breakaway drills are an afterthought. When kids practice shooting, they go one-on-one or even one-on-two, because that's the way it happens in a game. Sometimes we'll give the player the puck at center ice and send him away with another player in

Why does Phil Esposito lead the NHL in goal scoring just about every year? Here's one good reason. Phil has wedged himself between Peter Mahovlich and the Montreal goaltender and now is in perfect position to take the corner pass-out that is almost certain to come. Once he gets the puck, Phil usually snaps it into an open corner of the net before the poor goaltender can even react.

pursuit. That way we combine shooting with backchecking. Kids must learn to shoot with pressure on them. How often do you break in alone down the right wing in a game? Why not make the shooter practice trying to beat a defenseman *and* the goaltender? So don't make it easy on yourself. I remember vividly that the Russians could have three and four Team Canada players draped all over them, yet they still got off their shot. They prepared themselves to play hockey the way it is played during a game.

In working with young hockey players, I try to take the basic teaching points of the game and adapt them to the particular talents of each player. For instance, if a twelve-year-old right wing has a great wrist shot but shoots the puck from the heel of the blade rather than the middle, I don't tell him he is 100 percent wrong and make him learn to shoot it from the middle. Do you think I'm about to tell Phil Esposito that he doesn't put his bottom hand far enough down the shaft on his wrist shot? Jack Nicklaus uses one type of grip, while Arnold Palmer uses another. Roger Maris and Mickey Mantle had different stances. Ted Williams batted left-handed, while Roberto Clemente batted right. There is no definitive way to play hockey.

So practice. Get an old piece of playwood. Go down to the garage. Nail a goal-sized target to the back wall. And shoot.

As I line up a slap shot during pregame practice, the puck rests flat and stationary on the ice. Body weight is moving forward as I take the stick back, but the weight will be all forward at impact.

Overleaf: Thigh power is the key ingredient to good skating. My weight is forward, and having the leading knee well bent enables me to generate a full, powerful stride. I also work my arms, much like a sprinter, to get my whole body into the stride.

The Game in Color

On the following pages, Heinz Kluetmeier's cameras capture the speed, the color, the action, and exquisite technique of Orr executing hockey's basic moves. Here too is Orr in action against the Montreal Canadiens, the Philadelphia Flyers, and other NHL teams, along with photographs showing the styles of other hockey greats.

In these pictures, Walter Tkaczuk of the Rangers, Yvan Cournoyer of the Canadiens, and I are moving at good speed around the ice. Our styles are different but, most importantly, our heads are up.

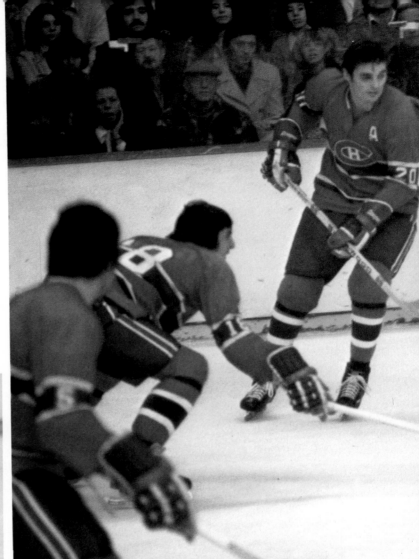

Good skaters must master sharp turns. Above right, I pivot abruptly to avoid the Montreal players who have hemmed me in temporarily. Left, Yvan Cournoyer is turning so fast he seems to be riding the boots of his skates—not the blades. And at the right, Walter Tkaczuk and I look as though we're competing in the Men's Pairs as Tkaczuk wheels away with the puck and I follow him into the play.

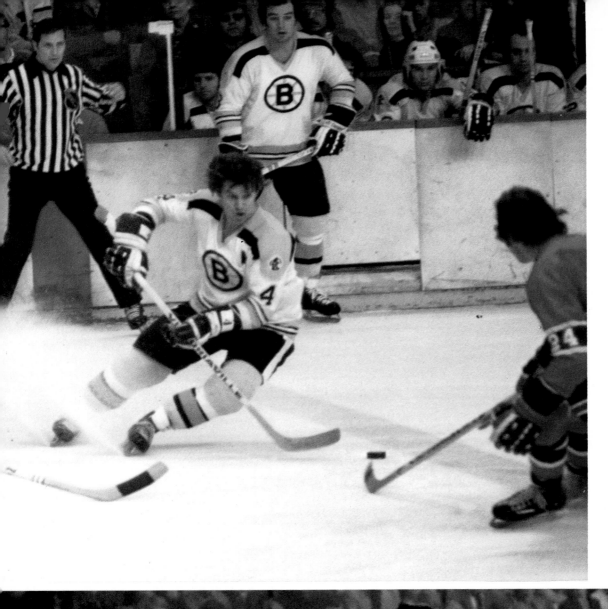

I try to keep the puck well in front of me while stickhandling (below), using gentle sweeps rather than violent thwacks. However, as you see in the picture on the right, there is still plenty of opportunity to deke the defender, using my head and hips.

When firing a wrist shot (bottom), I get forward of the puck by circling until it is in a position slightly behind my left foot. As I sweep the puck forward, my wrists are cocked, my head is over the puck, and my weight low, moving to the front. As I release the puck, I rise into the shot rolling my wrists under — not over — and follow through naturally toward my intended target (top right). Occasionally we all must violate the basic rule of good shooting technique and fire away off the wrong foot, as I happen to be doing in the insets.

I am balanced and ready to
release my "quick" slap shot.

Uncoiling a slap shot.

Yvan Cournoyer puts his head almost to the ice and drops his bottom hand almost onto the blade of the stick when he powers his slap shot (right). My back foot floats in midair and my weight shifts onto my right foot as I release my slap shot (bottom).

The essence of hockey: the shooter against the masked man in the goal. Here, the goaltender comes out on me to cut off the angles, but a quick flip shot takes a good bounce.

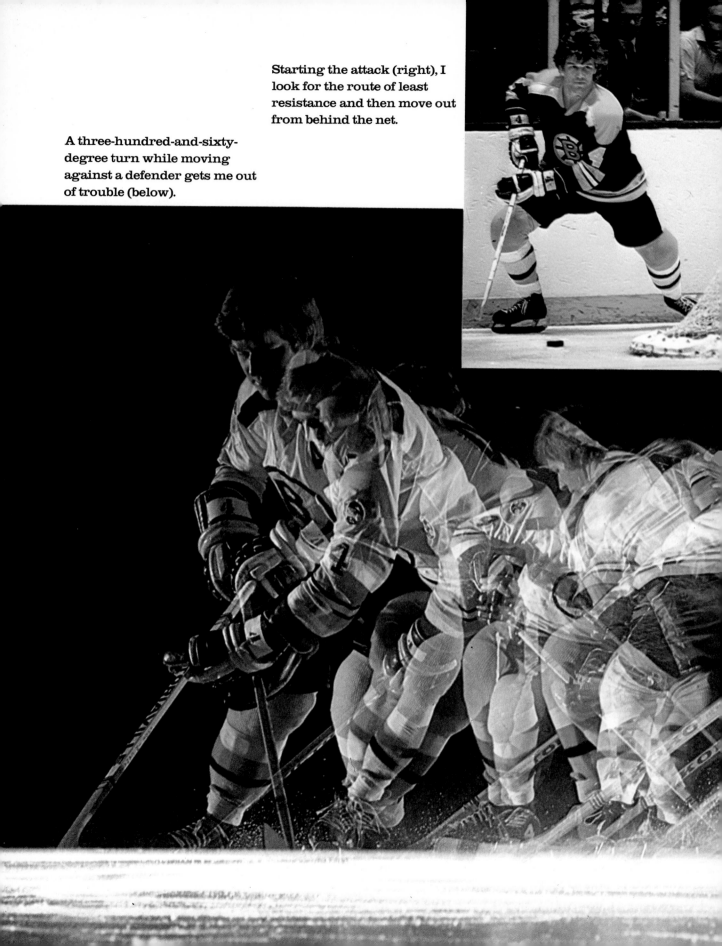

Starting the attack (right), I look for the route of least resistance and then move out from behind the net.

A three-hundred-and-sixty-degree turn while moving against a defender gets me out of trouble (below).

As I cross through center ice (right), Phil Esposito skates away to get open for a possible pass.

Behind the opponents' net (above), I keep the puck well in front of me and use my arms and body to fend off rival defensemen.

When players like Bobby Clarke of the Philadelphia Flyers (top left) control the puck, the job of the defenseman gets very complicated.

"Positioning" is the key word during activity around the net. The defenseman must keep himself between his goaltender and the rival players at all times, as I happen to be against Bobby Rousseau of the Rangers (bottom left) and Paul Henderson of Toronto (below).

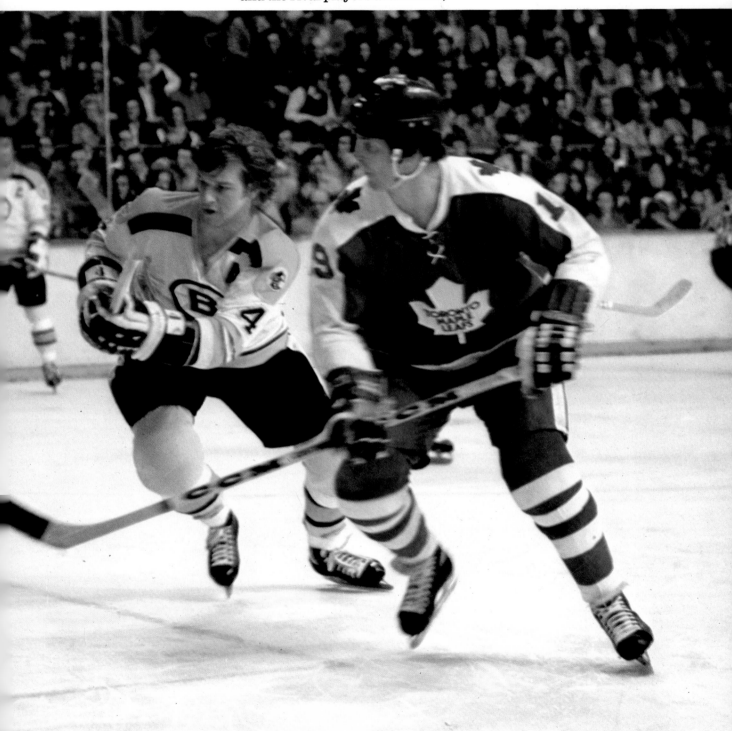

The best way to block a shot is to drop to one knee, as in the strobe photograph, but there are many times when I must drop to both knees to stop a shot before it reaches my goaltender — as I am doing against Walter Tkaczuk — which means I'm momentarily immobile, with Tkaczuk free to go for any rebound.

Caution: when you go down to block a shot, make certain that you are in position to do some good. Here, I am too far out of the shooter's line.

CHAPTER FIVE

Attacking

All top teams in all sports operate with a particular attacking philosophy. In some cases management dictates the philosophy and finds the players to fit it. For instance, the Montreal Canadiens have always been a "skating" team and have mastered the so-called "headmanning the puck" style of offense; consequently, the players they acquire by draft or trade are usually superior skaters and passers. In other cases the talents of individual players determine the approach. The Boston Celtics, for example, were just another basketball team until Bill Russell arrived at the Boston Garden in 1956. With Russell swallowing up all the rebounds and sending the Cousys, Sharmans, Havliceks, Joneses, and Heinsohns fast-breaking up the court, the Celtics immediately became the greatest dynasty in the history of pro basketball. Sometimes the dimensions of a playing field, local weather conditions, or some other factor decides the manner in which a team plays its game. The Los Angeles Dodgers have been a Punch-and-Judy type of baseball team and have survived almost exclusively with exceptional pitching ever since moving into Dodger Stadium in Los Angeles, mostly because the dimensions of the playing field cater more to bunts, stolen bases, and good pitching than to the long ball.

Since the start of the 1967–68 season the Bruins have played with one basic offensive system, too. The new Bruins—there were some twelve new players on our eighteen-man roster— were the biggest team in the league, strong, rough, and talented, and we played our home games on the smallest rink in the league. At the time, Harry Sinden put in a five-man attacking system that originated from the defense and emphasized bodychecking and puck control. It is the style we still use today. We are a patient team, to say the least. We don't panic. And it works. Besides two Stanley Cups, three first-place finishes, and one tie for first place in the seasons from 1967–68 through 1973–74, the best indicator of the success of that attacking philosophy is our cumulative record for those years on our home ice at Boston Garden. In fact, we lost only thirty-three of two hundred and thirty regular-season games at the Garden in six years, then in the 1973–74 season we played twenty-two games at the Garden before finally losing there for the first time. We must be doing something right.

Defense or Offense?

I have been called a lot of printable and unprintable names by people during my career, but the only time I get really mad is when someone calls me a "rover." They say, "Orr's not a defenseman, he's a rover," and, boy, I could go through the roof. Let me set the record straight right here. I'm not a rover. Or a center forward. Or a center back. Or a flanker. Or even a designated attacker. In pure hockey terminology what I am is an "offensive defenseman." Get that? An offensive defenseman. In fact, I have been an offensive defenseman almost since I first started to play organized hockey as a six-year-old Squirt back in Parry Sound.

My reasons for becoming an offensive defenseman were to me very logical. As a kid I wanted to be on the ice as much as possible, and I always wanted to get the puck on my stick and rush up-ice with it. Defensemen work every other shift, while forwards work only every third shift. So defense was my position. Unlike the other defensemen, I didn't stand back and divorce myself from the attack. I got involved somehow. I carried the puck. I passed it. I shot it. I chased it down.

I suppose that Bucko McDonald could have permanently ended my career as a defenseman simply by moving me to center or the wing, but he never did. Bucko let me play my game. It has always been that way; indeed, none of my coaches in Parry Sound, Oshawa, or Boston has ever tried to change my style. No coach has suggested that I become a defensive specialist. Not yet, anyway. Oddly enough, when I signed my first pro contract with the Bruins in 1966, there was considerable speculation in Boston that they would try me at center ice in order to use, as they said, my "offensive talents to the fullest." It never happened, thank goodness, although I did play six or eight games at forward one year while I was recovering from another knee injury.

Although the purists may disagree, there certainly is nothing technically wrong with playing defense and still being part of the attack. Despite what my critics say, I'm not the first defenseman ever to get actively involved with his team's offense. People tell me Eddie Shore was a great rushing defenseman, and I know that Doug Harvey, Red Kelly, Pierre Pilote, and numerous other defensemen participated in, or in some cases even led, their team's attack. Also, it stands to reason that a team will hold a definite advantage over its rivals if and when it can involve four or even five players in the offense instead of the traditional three: the center and his two wings. Look at the Russian National Team. The Soviet attack is based on the assembly-line system and thoroughly employs all five skaters on the ice; in fact, the Soviet coaches place so much importance on the on-ice compatibility of the five players that they strictly rotate three five-man units while substituting during a game.

When I spot an opening, I accelerate

I suppose that I have helped to add an extra dimension to the role of the offensive defenseman by not limiting my rushes and by not terminating them at the opposition blue line. The great majority of defensemen in the NHL carry the puck to the blue line and then either pass it to a teammate or fire it into a corner, while the Russian defensemen tend to avoid the rushing approach completely and concentrate primarily on passing the puck to an open teammate. As far as I am concerned, the blue line is not red. It does not say "stop." If I get to that blue line and spot an opening ahead of me, I accelerate—not decelerate, as I will explain later in the chapter.

What many people seem to forget is that defensemen generally spot openings easier than forwards. Playing defense, remember, I always have the complete range of play contained within my vision. The game is right there in front of me. Forwards, on the other hand, must often skate with their backs to the play; they also must take passes or shots without knowing what's happening in other areas of the ice because they simply cannot see enough. The more I think about it, I realize that defensemen should always quarterback their team's offense, rather than avoid it, because defensemen and goaltenders have the best view of what's going on in a game. Don't forget those goaltenders, either. In Boston our goaltenders have always helped us by picking up our defensive and offensive mistakes, and by analyzing the other clubs' patterns and tendencies. I remember a Stanley Cup play-off game against the Toronto Maple Leafs a few years ago when Eddie Johnston interrupted play and signaled for me to come to his net, supposedly to help him remove some water or debris from around the goal mouth. Actually, all Eddie wanted to do was tell me that the player checking me on our power play always peeled away to my left *before* I unleashed my shot. I thanked him, then skated back up-ice to rejoin the power play. Sure enough, on the next face-off the puck rolled directly toward me, with the same checker in pursuit. I started through the motion of my slap shot, and in the middle of my takeaway I noticed that the checker had done exactly what Eddie J. told me: he had skated to my left, leaving me with a clear forty-five-foot shot at the goal. Instead of shooting, I collected the puck, wheeled to my right, moved closer to the net, and had an easy shot at the goaltender from about twenty feet out. He saved on my shot, but the rebound plopped down in the crease and another Bruin easily poked the puck into the net. Eddie J., of course, never got an assist on the goal, but he definitely deserved at least an asterisk.

I happened to arrive in the NHL at a time when the game of hockey was undergoing a complete change of image. In the old days, the six-team NHL featured mostly close-checking, low-scoring contests in which a total of forty shots on goal for both teams was considered unusually high. Then, in 1967, the NHL doubled its size to twelve teams and simultaneously we began to see many high-scoring shoot-outs in which each team took forty shots on goal. Now there are eighteen teams in the expanded NHL, and the offense dominates the defense in every way. Lord Stanley no doubt turned in his grave that May night in 1973 when the Chicago Black Hawks beat the Montreal Canadiens in a Stanley Cup play-off game by the improbable score of 8 to 7. The rival goaltenders in that game were not untested rookies; Chicago's Tony Esposito and Montreal's Ken Dryden were the league's two best goaltenders. Back in 1952 the late Terry Sawchuck scored four shutouts and allowed a total of only five goals in eight games as the Detroit Red Wings swept through the Maple Leafs and then the Canadiens to win the cup.

Today, even the goaltenders are getting into the offensive act. Ten years ago goalies touched the puck only in self-defense; now they chase the puck around behind the net, stop it, pass it up-ice, and get official "assists" on many goals. Goaltender Michel Plasse, who now plays for Kansas City, actually scored a goal one year when he played for a minor-league team in Kansas City. Plasse's team led by a goal in the final minute of play, so the other club removed its goaltender and replaced him with an extra shooter in an attempt to produce a tie. As the clock ticked away, Plasse made a save with his stick, controlled the puck, and fired it the length of the ice into the empty net. No goaltender has ever scored a goal in the NHL, although Eddie Giacomin came close one night when he hit the post in the closing seconds of a game against the Maple Leafs in Toronto. Believe me, I don't suggest hockey is quite ready for goal-scoring goaltenders. Of course, some purists still contend the game is not even ready for offensive defensemen.

The Wrong Side

I am a left-handed shot who plays right defense. Technically speaking, I play the "wrong side," since — according to the original book of hockey theory — left-handed shots should play the left side and right-handed shots should play the right side. So much for original theory. To my way of thinking, there is nothing wrong with playing the opposite side in a game. Yvan Cournoyer shoots left-handed but plays right wing for the Canadiens. Wayne Cashman, though he shoots right-handed, plays left wing in Boston for Phil Esposito and Ken Hodge on the highest-scoring line in hockey. Brad Park of the Rangers, Serge Savard and Guy Lapointe of the Canadiens, and Carol Vadnais of the Bruins all are among the many defensemen who shoot left-handed but play the right side. Over in Moscow, four of the five right wings and three of the four right defensemen on the Soviet National Team also play the "wrong side." So, for that matter, does the man they will never forget in Moscow: Paul Henderson, the right-handed shot who plays left wing for the Toronto Toros now. From the "wrong side," he destroyed the Russians by scoring game-winning goals in the last three games of the Team Canada matches, including the series-winning goal with just thirty-four seconds to play in the eighth and final game. Except for Henderson and Cashman, though, most of the "wrong side" players are left-handed shots who work either at right wing or right defense.

For some strange reason, at the present time there are considerably more left-handed shots than right-handed shots playing hockey. In the NHL, roughly three of every four defensemen and three of every five forwards shoot left-handed. In Russia sixteen of the eighteen forwards and seven of the eight defensemen on the National Team shoot left-handed. The Bruins, for instance, had thirteen left-handed shots and only six right-handed shots on their 1973–74 roster. In that same season Boston, Montreal, and New York — the three top teams in the NHL's East Division — did not use even one right-handed shot as a regular defenseman. Twenty years from now, though, the situation probably will be reversed, much as it was in baseball. Five or six years ago baseball officials were lamenting the lack of good young catchers in their game. Suddenly Johnny Bench, Thurmon Munson, Ted Simmons, Carlton Fisk, and Ray Fosse all arrived in the big leagues, and now those same officials are wondering where all the third basemen went.

While the disadvantages of playing the "wrong side" far outnumber the advantages, I think the significance of the advantages far outweighs the disadvantages. One major problem is the trouble I always encounter when trying to take the puck off the boards on my backhand side. Another is that I must *make* and *take* more passes on my backhand than I ordinarily would like. And I must carry the puck much closer to the checkers than I'd like while going up the right side on a rush. The backhand, remember, is every player's weak side, including mine. One slight advantage of playing the "wrong side" is that occasionally players clearing the puck will forget that I play the "wrong side" and try to shoot the puck out through the middle of the ice, rather than along the boards. When that happens I am usually in excellent position to intercept their clear-out with my forehand and get off a quick shot or a quick pass. The very major advantage, though, is that I have a better angle for my shots at the goal. The way I calculate it, by shooting left-handed instead of right-handed from the right defense area at my blue line, I always shoot the puck from a position about twelve feet closer to the center of the ice than a right-handed defenseman would. The closer I get to the center of the ice, the better the angle, and the more openings I will have at the goal. To me, this is like finding money.

I'm not suggesting that coaches everywhere take their ten-year-old kids with left-handed shots and turn them into right wings or right defensemen. Kids have enough problems at that age learning how to skate properly and to grasp the fundamentals of the game. Don't make it any harder for them. But once they show an awareness of the fundamentals and seem capable of handling the tricky skating maneuvers, don't hesitate to change them to the "wrong side" if that seems desirable for the team. As I said, there's nothing wrong with the wrong side.

Audibling a Rush

Fundamentally, the shortest distance between two points is a straight line, but hockey is hardly a game of fundamental logic. If you take twelve players, put them out on a two-hundred-foot by eighty-five-foot rink, and drop down a small puck, then the shortest distance between any two points becomes a serpentine route filled with extreme hazards. Hockey, you might say, is like a downtown expressway during the rush hour. You must go where the openings are. As I have stated repeatedly, hockey is a game of openings. There is no grand master plan for scoring goals. We don't huddle behind our net and call a play: "OK, 27 Wing Left Counterflex Spread Trap Fleaflicker Blitz on Two, Double Hut"—and then try to set up Phil Esposito as he breaks behind the right defenseman. Although if Phil does manage to break behind the right defenseman, and if there's an opening on the ice between Phil's position and mine, I will try to get him the puck with great haste. Oftentimes, though, forwards appear to be in the open but, in fact, they actually are not, because there is no way for the puck carrier to get the puck to them. When that happens, I simply look for an opening somewhere else. I audible.

I don't know how many audibles are called during a rush, since the number of audibles necessarily varies according to the particular alignments of all the other players on the ice. This may sound wrong, but I doubt that I make two identical rushes during any single period. I cannot divulge any special or secret tactics for making the superperfect rush up-ice every time because there simply is no one special or secret key to offensive hockey. My rush is one great option play as I look for openings. There is, however, a definite way to begin a rush. Before I even think about carrying the puck up-ice, I organize myself. I assess the total picture in front of me and plan accordingly.

Perhaps it would be best to break down a rush into five major sections: (1) setting up; (2) breaking out; (3) decision at the red line; (4) breaking in; and (5) beating the goaltender. As we begin, the other team has the puck and starts to skate out of its zone. Once across the center red line, the left wing fires the puck off the boards and down past me into the corner to the right of my goaltender.

Setting Up

No doubt I am skating backward when that rival left wing shoots the puck past me and into the corner. My first move, then, is a crisp crossover turn, swinging my left leg around and over my right and pushing away powerfully with the right, so that I can brake my backward motion, change direction quickly, and approach the puck head-on. Too many young players tend to avoid making the crossover turn and, instead, prefer to skate backward to where they *think* the puck will be in the corner. Bad. Suicide, in fact. Always approach the puck in a head-on way. As I step over to make my crossover turn, I take a quick look at the puck and develop a pretty strong feel for where it will be on the ice by the time I get to it. While crossing over I always look at the player who has just shot the puck into my zone and glance quickly at all the other players on the ice. In this particular situation the left wing tells me everything I want to know.

If he shoots the puck down the ice and then dashes toward his team's bench, I automatically know that a line change is in progress. When teams are changing their lines on the fly, they understandably are susceptible to a quick offensive strike because of the momentary confusion that line changes seem to

Strangely, most attacking maneuvers begin with a defensive tactic. In this sequence I am skating backward as the opposition controls the puck. When the puck is shot down the ice, I do a crossover turn and chase it back into the corner. If I get it, we're ready to start an attack of our own.

create. Say, now, the left wing *has* skated for his bench. Seeing this, I skate full speed toward the puck and collect it. Here the geography of the particular arena in which we are playing helps determine my next move. If the rival team's bench happens to be on the far side of the ice, I probably will pivot sharply and either pass the puck to an uncovered Bruin or skate back up the so-called "free" side of the ice; that is, the side farthest away from the rival team's bench, since that side will remain uncovered for a longer period of time than the side near the bench. However, if I get the puck in the right corner and the rival team's bench is on the same side of the ice, I undoubtedly will try to pass the puck to an uncovered teammate across the ice on the "free" side farthest away from the opposition's bench. In the Boston Garden, for instance, my right defense position happens to be on the same side of the ice as the visiting team's player bench during the first and third periods, but it is on the Bruins' side during the second period.

On the other hand, if the left wing shoots the puck down the ice and then chases after it, I automatically know that a line change is not in progress and that, in fact, the other team most likely is planning an all-out checking effort. Now, as I skate toward the puck, I keep turning my head from side to side, looking over my shoulders in an attempt to determine: (1) the positions of the checkers coming from my right; (2) the position of the puck; and (3) the positions of the left wing and any other players skating at me from my left. These quick glances decide, for the most part, what I hope to accomplish — and how I accomplish it — during the next ten or twelve seconds, or at least until we

get a good scoring opportunity at the other end of the ice.

As a general rule, opposing teams normally employ three types of checking tactics in situations where a player is pursuing a puck in the corner near his own net. Since I never know what particular checking tactic a team will use against me until perhaps a second or two before I touch the puck, I can hardly approach the puck with any preconceived play in my mind. Indeed, as strange as this may sound, the checkers really dictate my moves. And I must react instinctively to execute them. Here is a rundown of those three checking tactics, as well as what I usually must do against them in order to keep control of the puck for the Bruins.

1. The opposition may send only one man in deep against me; probably the left wing who shot the puck into the corner and who is now closer to the puck than any of his teammates. As I turn my head from side to side, I hope to be able to detect this particular checking strategy. Once I get the puck, I will do one of two things, depending upon the closeness of the checker and the enthusiasm with which he is checking me. For instance, if the checker is approaching me at full speed and obviously intends to slam me against the boards, hoping that the puck will squirt loose and be picked up by one of his teammates, I most likely will fire the puck around the boards behind the net to my defense partner, who should be coming back down the ice, too. If things are going really smoothly, that left defenseman will be trailed by our left wing. In other words, there should be two Bruins ready to pick up the puck when it reaches the other side of the ice. When this succeeds, I temporarily trap the checking player

The perfect starting position for an attack: my seat practically rests against the boards behind the net, where I can scan the complete rink looking for openings.

deep in the zone and create an important manpower advantage for my own team as we skate back up-ice with the puck.

However, if that same left wing is simply chasing me in such a way that he obviously does not intend to run me into the boards, I will probably try to outskate him around the net and then head up the ice on the other side, with the checker skating in pursuit.

When I take off around the net, I always feel as though I have a distinct psychological advantage over that trailing checker. While I am just beginning my move, the attacking play, he actually has just completed his, the forechecking maneuver, and has failed to do his job. Psychologically, I have an advantage over the checker. When I turn the net and skate away, I always feel as though the ice is sloped downhill and there's a fifty-mile-per-hour wind at my back. On the other hand, when a checker turns the net and skates back up-ice, he is convinced that the ice is all uphill, like climbing the side of a mountain. Whatever the feeling, I figure that I can pick up as many as two or three strides on a trailing checker while I skate from my net to the red line at center ice.

2. The opposition may send that same left wing in deep against me and then double the coverage by having the center approach me from the opposite direction, usually by skating down *his*

The right side is the right side out in this situation, as Garnet Bailey of the St. Louis Blues skates around the Boston net in an attempt to check me into the boards. Phil Esposito spotted Bailey's maneuver, though, and skated back toward the net to help me out (bottom left). Seeing Bailey trapped behind the net, Al Sims — my defense partner — cleared a lane by moving well to the left and I suddenly had an opening up the middle of the ice (below).

right side and swinging behind the net in an attempt to head me off. Double trouble, you might say. I should be able to spot this checking tactic while looking from side to side as I skate toward the puck. If I do spot it and beat it, I undoubtedly will give my own team a glittering opportunity for a goal because I will have trapped two rival players deep in the zone, not just one. What I do in this situation is very basic, although it requires steady nerves in that I must hold onto the puck until the last possible moment—or else I will probably ruin that glittering scoring opportunity for my team. Once I get the puck in the corner, I wheel around to avoid the checkers—all the while still looking for an uncovered teammate. In most instances I will look first for my *own* right wing, who should have trailed the rival left wing down toward the corner. After that I will look toward the back of the net, where my defense partner should be stationed. And then I'll look over to the far corner to see if my left wing has come back to help out, too. All this happens in a few seconds, even though it may sound endless. The puck will go to the *open* teammate who is in the best position to break down the ice. This normally means that I will pass the puck to my right wing. He generally is open, since the rival left wing is pursuing me and the rival left defenseman does not dare advance too deeply into the zone, and, better yet, he usually is closer to me and the puck than any of my other teammates. So, having wheeled, I wait until the rival checkers are practically on top of me, then I pass the puck to that *open* teammate. I try to pass the puck off the boards, thus minimizing the risk of losing it because of a bad pass. A bad pass directed toward the middle of the ice oftentimes results in a goal for the opposition. However, a bad pass off the boards is usually just a bad pass, which is unfortunate but not necessarily a disaster. As I release the puck I probably will be sandwiched by the rival checkers. Good! The longer they remain involved with me, the more time my own team will have to set up a good scoring opportunity at the other end of the rink. Too many players, I'm afraid, take a kamikaze attitude when they are confronted by two forecheckers in a corner. Rather than take the safe and easy way out by making a short pass to a teammate, they try to skate out of the corner with the puck themselves. Believe me, don't ever be stupid enough to try that in a game. There is no doubt that the two checkers will steal the puck from you and quickly move in for a good scoring chance—and probably a goal—against *your* goaltender. When two rival players are converging on you, the *only* way you can beat them is by passing the puck to an open teammate. At least, that's the sensible thing to do.

3. The opposition simply may decide not to check me too closely and, instead, try to blanket the zone with its three forwards in an attempt to seal off all possible escape routes. In fact, most

teams in the NHL—apparently fearful of getting burned by having one or two of their checkers trapped too deep in the zone—usually let retreating defensemen or forwards take the puck and skate behind their own net with it. But as far as I am concerned, when I am standing behind my net with the puck there on my stick, I am in the safest position on the rink. It is from this behind-the-net position that the Bruins initiate most of their attacking plays.

Breaking Out

Stop and look! Once I stop behind my net with the puck, I don't take a quick, aimless glance to see what's happening on the ice. I look. I look. And I look again. Then I may take still another look. Most young players, I'm afraid, are very headstrong when it comes to breaking out of their own zone with the puck. They skate behind their net, pause momentarily for a perfunctory glance around the ice, and then break away in some direction, any direction. At no time do they give any real thought to the particular defensive tactics currently being employed by the opposition, and, even worse, they never bother to analyze the respective positions of their teammates. The plan, as they dream it, is that they will skate up the ice, cut around the center, move inside the right wing, split the defense, pull the goaltender down with a combination head-and-knees fake, and then flip a backhander into the top left corner of the net. Great, if they can do it. Trouble is, the players who try to make such plays all the time now live in the minor leagues, or on a bench. As I have said repeatedly, there are no preplanned plays in the game of hockey.

There are a number of excellent reasons for initiating plays from that behind-the-net position. For one thing, as I stand there, I have a perfect overview of everything and everyone on the ice. Thus, I am in the best position to spot *openings*. For another, by stopping the flow of play for a second or two, I give my teammates a chance to get reorganized and set into position for the attack. Third, since I don't know whether I will skate out to my left or to my right until I actually do it, I compound the problems facing the defensive players in our zone. If I don't know what I'm going to do, they certainly don't know and, as a result, must be prepared for anything and everything.

As I stand there behind the net, I practically rest my seat against the boards and keep the puck squarely in front of me. Many young players develop the bad habits of either standing too close to the back of the net or of keeping the puck to one side. Some players stand too close to the net *and* keep the puck to one side. The closer you stand to the net, the tougher it will be for you to maneuver with the puck when you begin to break away; in fact, you may bounce the puck against the bottom of the net and lose control of it. And if you keep the puck too far to one side while you stand behind the net, you definitely will tip your intentions to the checkers and make their jobs considerably easier. For instance, if I hold the puck out on my left side, say a foot or two outside my left skate, chances are that I will either skate out that side or pass the puck up that left side. Defensive players do not have to be geniuses to figure that out.

So now I am standing behind my net, with the puck positioned squarely in front of me, and I'm looking and looking and looking up the ice. Once again, what I do next depends strictly on the positions and the tactics of the rival checkers. In these defensive situations NHL teams normally place their lead checker, the center, at the edge of the crease and station their wingmen out near the sideboards, relatively close to the offensive wingmen. While it is impossible to forecast with any accuracy what lead checkers will do every time, they generally tend to fall into predictable patterns. Dave Keon of the Toronto Maple Leafs is one of the best skaters in hockey. He usually hops around the edge of the crease, waits for me to skate out, and then closes in with some excellent forechecking. Keon is so fast and so quick that the only real way I can expect to beat his forechecking is by working a give-and-go pass play with one of my teammates. I rarely, if ever, try to outskate a Keon in *my* zone. Neither Walt Tkaczuk of the New York Rangers nor Bobby Clarke of the Philadelphia Flyers are as fast or as quick as Keon, but they are much stronger than Keon and like to use their bodies and sticks on me. Again, the best way to avoid the Tkaczuks and the Clarkes is to work a give-and-go pass play with a teammate.

The defenseman is the "boss" on all breakout plays from behind the net and must always control the movement of the puck.

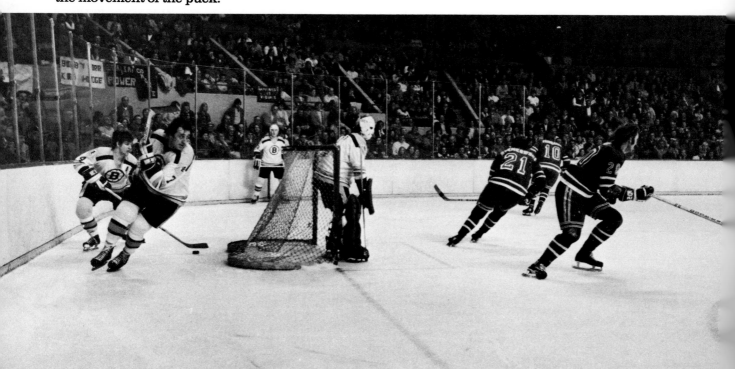

These two are among a number of aggressive checkers in the NHL—a group that also includes Don Luce of Buffalo, Pete Stemkowski of the New York Rangers, and Dennis Hextall of the Minnesota North Stars—who like to charge around behind the net in an attempt to pin the puck carrier against the boards, tie up the puck, and get a face-off. Of course, when they do that, they can skate behind the net from only one side—either the right or the left—and thus leave a large gap on the other side. Still, the element of surprise—after all, who expects a checker to come behind the net?—oftentimes confuses the puck carrier so much that he will either lose the puck outright or have it tied up for a face-off. In recent years I have developed sort of a cat-and-mouse routine in an attempt to discourage these surprises.

When that lead checker charges around behind the net, I abandon my position and skate out the other side—crouching and bending in such a way that my head is below the top of the net—and then promptly cut directly in front of my goaltender and return to my starting position behind the net. Meanwhile, the checker, frustrated by his lack of success and thinking that I have skated up the ice, probably has put his head down, churned his legs, and taken off up the ice to *rejoin* the play. The puck carrier always has an advantage in a small area with the net for a shield.

Surprises aside, getting the puck from behind my net to the red line at center ice is a tricky and at times very demanding assignment. The defenseman is the quarterback, charged with calling the correct audibles at the correct times. Every move I make is based on instinct, tempered by experience. Or to put it another way, the moves I make are executed instinctively as a result of the moves the opposition checkers have made in reaction to the moves I myself have previously made.

Stated simply, all I do is take the route of least resistance, regardless of how many detours I have to make. If I am not impeded by checkers, I can skate from behind my net to the red line in three or four seconds. But if checkers are swarming all over the zone, as usually is the case, it may take as long as twenty, twenty-five, or even thirty seconds and five or six passes to get the puck from that safe spot behind the net to the red line.

Organization is the key to a successful breakout play, and it starts with the proper positioning of the soon-to-be attacking players. When I stand behind my net with the puck, my defense partner should be stationed in front of the net and my two wingers should be out along their respective boards, somewhere between the top of the face-off circle and the blue line. My center, though, is on his own. We have always had great playmaking centers in Boston: Esposito, Sanderson, Fred Stanfield, and now Gregg Sheppard and André Savard. They all understand the

A

In this breakout sequence, I said "No, no," to center Gregg
Sheppard as he came behind the net to possibly take the
puck (A) and decided that I should carry the puck behind
Gregg out to the right side (B). However, New York center
Jean Ratelle (19) reacted perfectly and moved to seal off the
opening I had spotted on the ice (C).

D

So with Ratelle and Vic Hadfield (11) closing down that
right side, I suddenly had to forget about Sheppard
and look for a new opening (D). Al Sims was isolated on
the far left side of the ice (E), so I turned and passed the
puck to him and then skated over to follow him out (F).

B

C

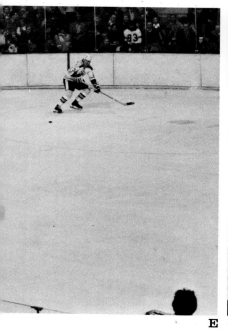

E

F

The perfect tandem breakout play. I held the puck behind our net and scouted the ice for openings as Phil Esposito (7) began to skate around the net (A). I decided to take the puck out myself (B), and Esposito swung wide to my right for a possible pass (C).

A

The New York wingers retreated to cover their wings, but Ranger center Pete Stemkowski moved in to forecheck against me (D). Seeing this, I passed the puck to Esposito (E), and as we skated up-ice Stemkowski was trapped in our zone (F).

D

B

C

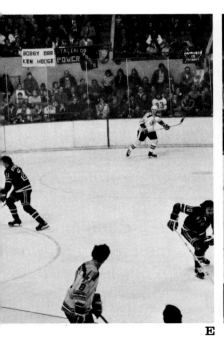

E

F

necessary give-and-take, take-and-give rapport that must exist between an offensive defenseman like myself and a center iceman in order for an attack to work successfully. For instance, Phil Esposito sees me behind the net, sees the positions of the checkers, and instinctively decides that I can skate the puck out myself; so he, in turn, should start breaking for center ice. Or maybe he sees me behind the net, sees the positions of the checkers, and decides that I won't be able to get the puck out by myself, that I need help. Then he comes back behind the net and breaks out in tandem with me.

When breaking out, the defenseman is the boss

The tandem breakout play is very safe and usually very productive. It works like this: I have the puck behind the net, of course, and I am studying the options available to me. Meanwhile, the center is either skating with his back to the checkers or moving along the end boards, which means that he does not have a broad view of the obstacles confronting us. Consequently, I make the final decision on whether the center or I will start out with the puck. If, for example, the center is coming from my right and there happens to be a checker ten feet away on my left, I certainly will not let him take the puck out. Instead, I will let him lead the way, and he will either skate interference for me against the rival checker or skate into an open position for a short pass. But if the center is coming from my right and the left side is wide open, I most likely will give him the puck and then follow him out that same left side. I never make this important decision until the last possible moment, so the center always must be alert. If I want him to take the puck, I'll say either "yes, yes, yes" or "take it, take it, take it" as he approaches me and carefully move the blade of my stick back away from the puck to avoid any confusion. If I don't want him to take the puck, I'll say "no, no, no" or simply hide the puck from him with the blade of my stick. Remember, the defenseman is the boss here, not the center, and communication is imperative. In these tandem breakout plays, the defenseman and the center never should stray too far from each other for mutual security reasons. When the center takes the puck out from behind the net, I always follow on his heels in the event that he encounters trouble from the opposition and must dispose of the puck pronto. And when I skate out with the puck, I always expect the center to be close by in case I meet with trouble. In fact, the breakout play we seem to use most often with the Bruins is a tandem maneuver with countless give-and-go and drop passes between the defenseman and the center.

Let's say, though, that my center has surveyed the situation and has decided not to skate behind the net. Well, here I go. Where? Wherever my instinct tells me to go. I start to skate, moving to my left or my right depending upon the positions of the checkers. I go for an "opening," wherever it is. As I start out, I try to skate in the middle of the ice, to give myself the maximum number of options for my audibles, as a puck carrier and as a passer. For instance, if I encounter problems with a checker, I can avoid him by skating to either my right or my left; I can't be hemmed in. If I want to pass the puck, I can move it left to my left wing, right to my right wing, straight ahead to my center, or even backward to my trailing defense partner. Consider, on the other hand, the lack of options available to me if I favor one side of the ice as I break out. If I go up the right wing, for instance, I certainly cannot try any risky cross-ice passes to my left wing; I probably will have to use the boards to get a pass to my right wing; and I most likely will be able to pass the puck only to the near side—the right side—of my center. What really happens is that when I skate up one side of the ice, I reduce the involvement of teammates on the other side in any plays that might develop.

While I am skating up the middle of the ice, I am looking, looking, looking—and not at the puck on my stick. Openings. I want to find openings. Don't be stupid and think you can get the job done yourself, as I have been in the past and no doubt will be in the future. As the cliché goes, there is no "I" in TEAM. If the left wing is open, he gets the puck. If the center is open, he gets the puck. If the right wing is open, he gets the puck. One of the first big words I learned back in Parry Sound was "teamwork," a big word for a six-year-old in the first grade. Be flexible as you move up the ice—not stupid—and always try to hit the open man.

Decision at the Red Line

I'm not a defensive defenseman. I like the puck. I like to carry it. Most defensemen in the NHL rarely, if ever, carry the puck much beyond the red line at center ice because they fear that they might get trapped up-ice and cost their team a goal. They know they are defensemen, not offensemen. In Russia, for instance, the defensemen are strictly feeders; in the entire eight-game Canada-Russia series in 1972 I don't believe the Soviet defensemen attempted more than a half-dozen rushes into our zone by themselves. That's not for me, thank you. If I still have

the puck on my stick when I reach center ice, the chances are about eighty to twenty that I will keep skating forward and try to be an active participant in the attacking play. Depending once again on the "openings" available to me as a result of the on-ice positions held by the opposition players as well as my own teammates, I will instinctively audible any one of a number of possible decisions.

1. As I look around for openings, I may notice through my peripheral vision that one of my wingers is busting down his lane a stride or two ahead of his checker and also a stride or two ahead of me. If I try to advance the puck across the blue line myself, I no doubt will cause an offsides play because that winger already will have preceded me—and the puck—over the line. So, instead, I will fire the puck across the blue line and into the corner for which my winger is headed. He definitely should be able to control the puck. For one thing, he already has that extra step or two on his checker. For another, while he is barreling full speed toward the corner, the rival defenseman on his side of the ice has been skating backward and now, seeing the puck shot into the corner behind him, must turn quickly, motor up, and then charge for the corner himself. Being a defenseman myself, I can assure you that this is usually a pretty hopeless mission.

All systems were "go" when we reached the blue line on this attacking maneuver. We were all onside and both my left wing and my center were open for passes. I also had plenty of skating room. The key to situations such as this is that the attacking players must have a rapport with the puck carrier and must not — repeat not — skate offside.

2. I may notice that one of those rival defensemen looks as though he wants to come across toward me and try to body me out of the play. If this is what he'd like to do, great. In fact, I'll try to help him out. What I'll really do is lure him into thinking I am not aware of his intentions and try to sucker him into taking a run at me. Sure, he may hit me. By running at me, though, he automatically leaves a large gap on his side of the ice. One of my teammates most certainly will spot that opening, and just before I get hit I will try to hit that teammate with a pass. If all goes well, we will end up with a breakaway on the goaltender.

3. I may notice that the defensemen are backing up into their zone and therefore leaving me with a lot of penetration room. If they are backing up, I most likely will carry the puck into the zone myself and then search out the next opening.

4. I may notice that the rival defensemen and forwards — all five of them — are stacked up at the blue line in barricade fashion. The New York Rangers like to employ this type of defensive strategy against us. When this happens, I'll either fire the puck through the cracks in the barricade and let my forwards chase it down into the corner; shoot the puck up along the boards so one of my wingers can tip it behind the defensive lineup in such a way that one of his linemates will be able to move in for a good scoring chance; or try to work a quick give-and-go play at the blue line with one of my open teammates. In the latter case, once I pass the puck to another Bruin, I will try to crash the barrier and streak for the net, hoping, of course, to get a return pass in the open. Stacking players at the blue line does provide some defensive advantages and eliminates certain maneuvers from an offensive team's repertoire; however, it also is very easy to trap the defensive players when they stay up there because, after all, there is no secondary layer of defense behind them.

5. I may not notice any "openings" at all. However, rather than give up control of the puck by attempting some impossible maneuver, I probably will turn around, retreat to about my own blue line, and then try it all over again. To repeat another hackneyed expression, if at first you don't succeed, try, try again.

Although I attempt to avoid the development of any predictable patterns of play in my approach to attacking, there is one thing that I rarely, if ever, do once I reach that center-ice area. I honestly cannot remember the last time I skated across the red line with the puck, fired it deep into the zone, and then chased after it myself. Why not? For a defenseman, such a play is total suicide. Let me explain. Defensemen who rush the puck frequently must have a solid on-ice rapport with their wingers, like mental telepathy. Wingers should be able to tell what a puck-carrying defenseman plans to do — and not botch up the play by skating offsides. More importantly, the wingers must decide which of them will stay back and cover for me at the blue line if

I take the puck into the zone and work in deep on the attack. Four players—that is, the attacking defenseman and his three forwards—should never be caught deep in the zone on a rush; one winger always must drop back and cover my point. Fortunately for me, this has never been a great problem in Boston, even though we do not have any standard rule that says "if Orr goes left, fakes right, cuts inside, spins around, falls down, and shoots the puck on his stomach, then the right wing drops back to the point." Wingers should always let their instinct guide them in these situations. At times the last winger trailing the rush should stay back to cover for me, particularly if he happens to be skating up the ice on the side farthest away from me. At other times the player on the opposite side of the ice should instinctively drop back if he feels that it will be easier for me to work a play of some sort with my close-by wing rather than try to involve him in what definitely would be a risky maneuver. And at other times—particularly when there are two or three defensive players bunched on the side of the ice where I am carrying the puck—the winger closest to me should drop back to the point, figuring that he will only create chaos by proceeding too far forward. So, having established this type of rapport with my wingers, I will only confuse them if I ever make the totally unexpected and indeed totally stupid play of shooting the puck into the corner and then tracking it down myself. Believe me, as I have learned the hard way, that is the best way to guarantee a two-on-one or a three-on-one break the other way for the opposition—and it is usually fatal.

Once I cross the blue line, skate into the zone, and dispose of the puck, I run through my mental checklist. First of all I immediately check to make certain that one of my wingers has dropped back to cover the point; if they both are barreling toward the goal, then I'll promptly remove myself from the attack and dash over to my normal defense position. If someone has covered for me, I'll survey the situation in front of me in an attempt to determine whether or not we will be able to maintain control of the puck in the attacking zone. If I think for even a second that we will lose control of the puck, I will look for the quickest way out of the zone and get ready for the inevitable attack against us. When all systems read "go," I then will streak for the net and hope for a pass-out from a teammate, a chance for a deflection of some player's shot, or a whack at a rebound.

Breaking In

Most times when I carry the puck into the zone, I will find myself facing a certain type of attacking situation. Suddenly it may be me against a lone defenseman—a one-on-one play, in other words. Maybe it will be a two-on-one play; that is, another Bruin and myself skating against a single defenseman. Or maybe it

Mano-a-mano. Someone gets faked out.
When attacking, I study a defenseman's eyes
and hope he'll tip me off about his intentions.
When defending, I study his chest because
he has to go where his chest goes.

Not all attacking plays work perfectly. Here, Phil Esposito
and I broke over the blue line against Detroit (A) and for
a fleeting moment it appeared that we had a good scoring
opportunity. I tried to cut in (B), but the backchecker and
the defensemen covered well (C) and forced me to the outside (D).

A

The third Detroit player covered Esposito closely (E) as I
went wide, and when it was all over (F), I was practically in
the corner, Phil was still well covered — and we had a busted
goal-scoring opportunity.

D

B

C

E

F

A

will be a three-on-two play; that is, two other Bruins and myself skating against two rival players, normally the two defensemen. In all these situations, of course, the goaltender is back there in his net, ready to provide a final line of resistance. Here are some of the things that run through my mind once these various situations present themselves while I am carrying the puck.

One-on-One: I don't study the moves rival players like to make. I don't have a *book* on defensemen or centers or wings that tells me what they will do 99.2 percent of the time when I move down against them at 13.74 miles per hour, fake left, cut right, push the puck through their legs, and then try to go around them and collect it. The same identical situations happen probably twice a season, or three times at the most. So keeping *books* is a waste of time. When I move in for a one-on-one, I simply want the other player to make the mistake—not me. If he seems to be moving backward too slowly, I'll probably try to put on a burst of speed and bust around him on whatever side I have the most room. If he seems to be moving backward at such a fast rate that he is unconsciously backing in on his goalie, I probably will try to skate as close to the defenseman and goaltender as possible and then fire a shot for whatever "opening" I see. According to an old hockey theory, you are not supposed to look at the eyes of another player when you are confronting him head-on; instead, you are supposed to stare at his chest. The reason, of course, is that a player can fake you out by moving his eyes in a thousand directions, but he definitely must go where his chest goes—unless he happens to be an elastic man. As far as I know, there are no

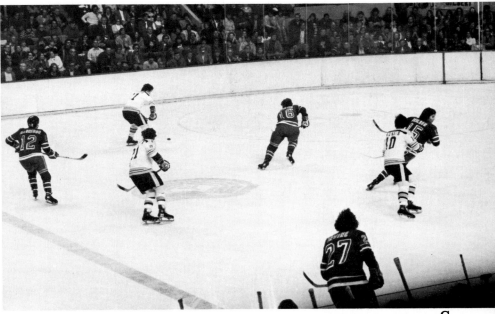

B

C

Carol Vadnais and Andre Savard worked a strong two-on-one against the Rangers as Vadnais lured defenseman Rod Seiling to one side (A) and slid a pass to the uncovered Savard (B), who then was in excellent position to either drop a pass to Don Marcotte (C) or take a shot himself (D). Savard decided that his best opening was a shot on goal (E), and he fired a blast at Eddie Giacomin.

D

E

elastic men playing hockey, though I wonder about Gilbert Perreault of the Buffalo Sabres at times. Also, by looking at someone's chest, you probably won't get suckered into a bad move. Nevertheless, despite what the old theorists say, when I carry the puck and move against a player, I look him right in the head. Right at his eyes. Those eyes will tell me everything I want to know. What I try to do is catch him looking the other way, worried, perhaps, that one of my teammates may be skating into position to join me on the play. His chest cannot tell me a thing because it never changes position. Once I see that the defensive player's eyes have wandered in another direction and have temporarily forgotten about me, I'm gone. My instinct propels me to the temporary *opening*, wherever it may be, that the defensive player has unconsciously created by peeking off in another direction. Of course, if he knows that I will make my move in reaction to what he does with his eyes, maybe he will try to fake me out by letting his eyes wander aimlessly in some direction and thus lure me into making a move that he is totally prepared for and, much to my amazement, ready to handle without any problems. What he does is give me a false sense of security, but there's nothing I can really do about it. Call it present shock. In all these one-on-one plays I always try to avoid the predictable; in fact, I oftentimes will try the near-impossible play rather than work the semibasic maneuvers that succeed perhaps every other time. For instance, say I happen to be skating down my right side against a lone defenseman. There are perhaps eight or ten feet between the defenseman and the boards to my right, but there are eighty feet between the same defenseman and the boards way over on the left side of the ice. So I will automatically go to my left, right? Maybe I will, but most times I will try to take the shortest and quickest route. In other words, I will try to go to my right and sneak between the defenseman and those near boards. I may get racked up into the boards, but it is worth the effort. Why? That defenseman expects me to skate to the wide side of the ice; that is, he figures I will go to my left and his right. His eyes most likely will tell me what he thinks. To help him out, I will fake to the wide side. Now he is convinced that I'm going wide. So it's a game of cat and mouse. As he goes wide, I go the other side, and by the time he catches on to what I am doing, I probably am already past him along the boards. On the other hand, as I mentioned earlier, he may be faking me out. I remember a game against the Chicago Black Hawks one night when I came down the boards against Bill White, one of the game's wiliest defensemen. As I looked at the whites of White's eyes, I noticed that he was looking to the wide side of the ice, apparently fearful that I would be moving to that wide side. So I went along with his eyes and faked to the outside myself, then darted to the inside. The next thing I knew, I was bouncing off the

From this angle my obvious play was a pass to winger Ken Hodge, who was standing alone next to Eddie Giacomin. However, a player who looks open from your angle is not necessarily open from my angle on the ice. Here, Hodge was uncovered, and I passed to him.

boards and crashing to the ice. I didn't fake White out. He faked me out. When I picked myself off the ice, I looked around for White. His head was down, but he raised his eyes at me and smiled. He smiled! I had to laugh myself. Hockey is a game of wits, and you don't win all the time. The thing is, you try to win more than you lose.

Two-on-One: The trick here is that the two attacking players must maintain their forward speed at a constant rate, or else their two-on-one suddenly will become a two-on-two or, even worse, a two-on-three. As the puck carrier, I try to get the lone defenseman to commit himself to a definite play before instinctively deciding what to do myself. In two-on-one plays the standard defensive rule is that the goaltender is responsible for the puck carrier while the defenseman is responsible for the other attacking player. Most times I will skate off to one side, thus forcing the defenseman to tip his hand. If he panics and comes after me, I will slide the puck across to my teammate, who then should have a clear shot at the goal. If he forgets me and covers my teammate, I will move in for a close shot at the goaltender. Another play I like to work in two-on-one situations is the drop pass. I will skate down the center of the ice, thus signaling my teammate that I want him to skate over and trail me down the middle. Once I drop the puck to him, I continue forward and try to obliterate the lone defenseman. By obliterate, I mean I try to either knock him out of the play or use him as a screen for the shot my teammate probably will take. Two-on-one situations oftentimes develop when a team is killing a penalty and catches the opposition with four men trapped too deep in the zone. Derek Sanderson and Eddie Westfall were the NHL's best penalty-killing team for years, and they used to work at least one short-handed two-on-one play in every game. When Sanderson teamed with Phil Esposito to kill many of our penalties, Derek and Phil patterned a very risky but highly successful two-on-one maneuver that drove rival defensemen and goaltenders daffy. Knowing that the defenseman is supposed to stay in the middle and the goaltender is supposed to handle the puck carrier, Derek and Phil created total chaos by skating down-ice fairly close to each other and passing the puck back and forth. The defenseman did not know what to do, and the goaltender was hung up with indecision. Phil might have shot the puck, Derek might have shot it. They didn't know, so how could the rival players have been expected to know? Whatever they ended up doing, though, it usually worked. However, while this may have worked for Derek and Phil, I don't recommend it for young players because of the split-second accuracy and timing that is required. Instead, young players should try to stay wide of the lone defenseman, force him to make his move, and then react accordingly. The advantage is yours — so don't blow it.

Three-on-Two: Without doubt this is the attacking play that develops most often during a hockey game: three players, usually the three forwards, breaking down against two players, usually the two defensemen. As an offensive defenseman, though, I participate in countless three-on-two plays in every game because, unlike most defensemen, I don't automatically dispose of the puck once I get to center ice. In the old days the players involved in the three-man attack always tried to work the puck to the man in the middle, usually the center, and let him make the play or plays. Nowadays there is no such unwritten rule; indeed, any of the three attacking players can act as the so-called playmaker. Once again there is no set maneuver that will always produce the desired effect—that is, a goal—in these situations. The key word, as always, is "openings." The puck carrier must search for openings—and then exploit them. However, there are a few basic maneuvers that you should perfect; once you do that, you will be able to work any number of variations off the basic plays. For instance, if I am the puck carrier on a three-on-two and happen to be skating down the wing, I like the man in the middle to drop back slightly and the man on the other wing to break for the goal mouth. By doing this I really create a two-on-two with a trailer effect. Consequently, I can either shoot the puck myself, knowing that the man in the center or the man on the wing will be available for a rebound; pass it to the streaking wing, who should be in good position for a tip-in goal; or simply drop the puck back to the man in the center, who should be open for a good shot on goal. However, if I am the puck carrier and happen to be skating in the middle of the ice, I like both my wings to break toward the net. By doing that they will occupy the attention of the two defensemen and let me skate very close to the goal before having to commit myself. Then I can either shoot the puck, pass it to my left wing, or pass it to my right wing, depending, of course, on the openings that developed as we broke toward the goal. I hate to keep repeating this but, again, I never preplan a move in situations such as this. I wait until the last possible moment to spot the best opening, then instinctively react to that opening. On the other hand, sometimes I am not the puck carrier on these three-on-two breaks. When that happens, I usually coast along a stride or two behind the puck carrier and the other Boston player, positioning myself for a drop pass or a good shot at a rebound.

In addition to these situations, there are countless other break-in plays—such as the three-on-one, the four-on-two, and the four-on-three—that occasionally develop during a game. Remember this: always look for the open man or the open shot. And if you are participating in a four-on-one, -two, or -three break, make certain that one of the four players on your team is in good position to get back on defense in the event the play backfires and the opposition, in turn, starts a play down the other way.

Beating the Goaltender

I don't study or analyze the moves goaltenders make to stop my shots, then draw up a grand scheme to beat them the next time I have the puck under the exact same conditions. In fact, the same conditions may never present themselves again. I don't know what I'm going to do with the puck until I get there. Where's *there?* I don't know, to be honest. *There* might be thirty feet out—or it might be right at the goal mouth. What I'm trying to get across, of course, is that you should not play hockey with any preplanned thoughts about what you're going to do. You play by instinct. Believe me, I've thought myself out of more goals than I care to remember. I remember we were playing the Detroit Red Wings one night, and the alleged scouting report on their young rookie goaltender—I think it was Doug Grant—was that he went for the first fake and was open for anything after that. Sure enough, early in the first game we played against the rookie I had a clear breakaway from center ice. As I skated in, I remembered what the scouting report had said about the goaltender. Instead of looking for an opening, I decided that I would fake him out. So I gave him my best head, shoulders, hips, and legs deke and expected him to fall all over himself. He stayed right there with me. I panicked and began to fake him again. Still, he never moved. Before I knew it, I had skated past the net and ruined a great scoring opportunity. And come to think of it, who can forget the scouting reports Team Canada received on Soviet goaltender Vladislav Tretiak before the start of the Canada-Russia series? Bob Davidson and John McLellan of the Toronto Maple Leafs flew to Moscow to scout the Soviets as part of the exchange agreement worked out between the two teams. Once in Moscow, Davidson and McLellan discovered that the Russian players were practicing in Leningrad, some four hundred miles away. The Russians dutifully put Davidson and McLellan on the overnight train to Leningrad. The local, naturally, not the express. In Leningrad the Russians immediately whisked Davidson and McLellan, who were understandably exhausted, to an exhibition game between the players who would be skating against Team Canada. From earlier reports Davidson and McLellan had been led to believe that Tretiak had an unbelievably poor glove hand—that he couldn't catch a basketball, let alone a flying puck. The results of that exhibition game completely confirmed those earlier reports. Tretiak gave up twelve goals, nine of them on his glove side, and when he did catch the puck, he juggled it nervously. Terrible glove hand, Davidson and McLellan duly noted, and that was the last they saw of Mr. Tretiak in Russia. However, unbeknownst to our scouts, Tretiak had been married two nights before that woeful exhibition and, in fact, had interrupted his honeymoon to play in the game. Also unbeknownst to our scouts, Tretiak had been spending ninety

hat you see is not always what
get. Goaltender Tony Esposito
the Chicago Black Hawks
ems to have left a generous
ening between his legs and a
rge gap to his left. But Tony
ways seals up openings very
uickly. He owns me, and I
ave scored only three or four
oals against him in the last
ve NHL seasons.

Moving in from the blue line with the puck, I had a number of alternatives, thanks to the maneuvering of Phil Esposito and Wayne Cashman. Esposito was in perfect position for a rebound or a deflection or even a quick pass as he moved around in the slot, while Cashman was shielding the goaltender, screening his vision of the play, and positioning himself for any rebound. I shot the puck—and it caromed off Cashman's stick and flew into the net.

minutes a day for the last four months catching pucks fired at him from all angles by an automatic shooting machine the Russians had purchased in—that's right—dear old Canada. Later, as it turned out, Tretiak's strongest attribute as a goaltender proved to be his unbelievably quick glove hand. In fact, it took us four or five games to discover that it did not pay to shoot the puck at Tretiak on his glove side. Well, so much for scouting reports on goaltenders.

Most times the man who wins the battle between the shooter and the goaltender is the man whose nerves hold out the longest. I want the goaltender to make the first move, thus presenting me with an opening. He wants me to make the first move. It's weird. I can panic. He can panic. Or we can end up in a stalemate. As a general rule, I look for the open shot and just shoot the puck. I prefer to shoot the puck low, too, but if I spot an opening somewhere else, I'll try to put it there. Shooters must play their individual strengths. For instance, I think I have a better chance to beat the goaltender by shooting the puck—not trying to deke him. On the other hand, players such as Gregg Sheppard, Gilbert Perreault, Stan Mikita, and Pete Mahovlich are such excellent puckhandlers and such excellent contortionists that they probably have a better chance to beat the goaltender by trying to fake him out of the net instead of just shooting the puck. Phil Esposito? Who knows. He's a great shooter and a great puckhandler. Whatever he does, the puck usually winds up in the net.

In my first eight years in the NHL, I scored on about 12.5 percent of the shots I put on goal. Not shots, mind you, but shots on goal. There is a difference. Considering the fact that I take a great majority of my shots from the thirty- to fifty-foot range, I think that my ratio of one goal for every eight shots is very respectable. Nevertheless, I am constantly baffled by goaltenders—their different styles, their different techniques, their different habits, their different everything. For instance, I always had better luck against Ken Dryden when he played for the Canadiens than I've had against Tony Esposito of the Black Hawks. Why? I don't know. I'm not saying that I was sorry to see Dryden retire and miss the 1973–74 season, but I always scored a few goals against him every year. Oddly enough, Dryden said back in 1971, shortly after his great play in goal helped the Canadiens upset us in the opening round of the Stanley Cup playoffs, that he thought I shot the puck low to his glove side too often. Maybe I did, maybe I didn't. I shot the puck for the openings I saw, and if he got his glove down to catch my shots—as he did in some of those play-off games but not in some others, because I did score the three-goal hat trick one night—then more power to him. Tony Esposito, though, owns me. I don't think I have scored more than three or four goals against him in the five years he has played for Chicago. He has a style all his own and flops all over the place. Better yet, he has great hands. I can't figure him out. Tony supposedly has a history of being weak on long shots from center ice, so occasionally I will flip a long, high shot at him and hope I get lucky. So far I never have. Oddly enough, the rest of the Bruins all have had better luck against Phil's brother than they had against Dryden. You figure goaltenders out. I can't.

As I mentioned, I try to keep my shots low, unless the goaltender's style obviously is more suited to low shots than high shots. For instance, I like to shoot high on Roger Crozier of the Buffalo Sabres because he crouches real low—almost putting his nose to the ice—and goes down in such a way that he covers most of the ice with his legs. I like to shoot high on Rogatien Vachon of the Los Angeles Kings, too, strictly because he is the shortest goaltender in the NHL and seems susceptible to shots fired at his shoulder level. In most circumstances, though, a low shot is the best, for four reasons: (1) a low shot has a better chance to go through a maze of players and into the net because, believe it or not, it is easier for a puck to whiz through twenty legs than ten bodies; (2) a low shot is tougher for the goaltender to see, even a croucher such as Crozier and a short man such as Vachon; (3) since a low shot is tougher to see, it also is much tougher for the goaltender to stop; and (4) since a low shot is tougher for the goaltender to stop, it is tougher for him to control the rebound—thus giving the attacking team a chance for another shot or two or three. Remember this, too. A goaltender can move his hands much quicker than he can move his feet. Ever put on a pair of goaltender's pads? I did one day—of course, I took them right off—and couldn't believe how heavy they felt on my legs. Late in a game I'm certain they must feel like a pair of iron doors to the poor, tired goaltenders. In shooting, I also try to be conscious of what hand the goaltender uses to catch the puck. All things being equal, I would much prefer to shoot the puck to his stick-hand side than his glove-hand side. The reasons are obvious: the goaltender cannot catch the puck with his stick hand, and he cannot move that stick hand as fast as he can move his glove hand.

When I shoot, I just want my shot to be on the net

However, when I shoot from my normal position near the right point, I never really worry about whether the shot will be high or low, glove hand or stick hand. I just want my shot—either a slap shot, which I use most of the time, or a wrist shot—to be near the net. If my shot is on the net, there is a chance it will beat the goaltender, either straight on or as the result of a deflection en route. And even if the goaltender stops my shot, he possibly will leave a rebound in front for one of my opportunistic teammates. Listen. When I shoot the puck from the point, I am not going to blow it past anyone very often. If an NHL goaltender has a clear view of my shot all the way, he will pick it off like a marshmallow. It gets to be like a game of catch for the goaltender; indeed, it's practically impossible to beat a good goaltender from sixty feet if he sees the puck all the way. When we play the Chicago Black Hawks, their defensemen work overtime to provide an open highway between Tony Esposito and me. To use a basketball term, they "pick" the Bruins who are near the goal and force them out of the lane between my position at the point and the net. As a result, Tony rarely loses sight of my shot—and we usually end up playing catch all night. The Russians, in fact, employed this same technique against Team Canada. Our players constantly protested to the officials that the Russians were guilty of interference when they "picked" around the net, but the complaints fell on deaf ears. The trick, of course, is for the attacking team to clog the front of the net, thereby harassing the goaltender and screening his vision. I'd much rather shoot into a crowd of players in front of the goal than play catch with the goaltender. Maybe the goaltender will never see the shot. Maybe it will be deflected en route. Maybe he will see it at the last moment, stop it somehow, and then leave an open rebound for one of my teammates. On the Boston power play, for instance, I know that Johnny Bucyk is parked—yes, parked—overtime at the corner of the net to the goaltender's right. I'm aware of that when I shoot, and I tend to shoot the puck in Bucyk's direction—knowing he will be there either to deflect the puck toward the goaltender or stop it and then flip it behind the goaltender.

Like all players, I guess, the scoring situation I like best is the breakaway. *Mano-a-mano*, the goaltender and me. I have no idea how many breakaways I have had in my NHL career, but I know that I have never used my slap shot on a breakaway. The slap shot is not a control shot, so why use it on a breakaway? Once again it comes down to a battle of nerves. Oddly enough, most goaltenders in the NHL, unlike most shooters, compile books on the shooting habits of their rivals, and they probably have a pretty solid idea of what you will do on a breakaway. So, once again, try not to type yourself. I like to skate head-on at the goaltender, not approach him from the side. By coming down the middle, remember, I give myself the maximum number of options, since I can go left or right—or even head-on. I wait for an opening. If I spot one, I will shoot the puck. If I don't spot one, I will try to create one. As far as I am concerned, I think the toughest move for a goaltender to stop is a play similar to that goal I scored against Glenn Hall of the St. Louis Blues in the overtime period of the fourth and final game of the 1970 Stanley Cup play-offs. Think of it this way. When I come down head-on at the goaltender and then move to one side, either the left or the right, the goaltender must move with me in that same direction. To move, the goaltender also must work his legs in such a way that he will leave a generous patch of open space between his right and left legs. Call that an *opening*. Sometimes it works, sometimes it doesn't. For me, though, it has been a very successful move.

Throughout the entire attacking rush, the dominant words are *audible, opening* and *control*. I audible to an opening and then strive to maintain control of the puck. The same situation prevails on the so-called *power play*, with extra emphasis on the word *control*. Most penalties in the NHL are for two minutes. In other words, the team with the power play will skate with a one-man advantage for two minutes, unless, of course, it manages to score a goal before the expiration of those two minutes. Unfortunately, too many teams think they have to score a goal during the first few seconds of their power play. As a result they take stupid risks, make terrible passes, and attempt impossible shots. What's the rush? If it takes a team one minute and fifty-nine seconds to score a goal on its power play, so what? Time doesn't matter on most power plays. The object is to control the puck in the attacking zone for as long as it takes to audible a pass to an open man or audible a shot to an opening in the goal. Remember, power play means that a team has a manpower advantage. Sooner or later one of the members of the power play should be able to get into an open, uncovered position for either a pass or a good shot. So don't rush it.

The Bruins have had the most potent power play in hockey for most of the last seven years. In 1969–70 we set an NHL record by scoring 81 power-play goals in 76 games—or more than one a game, a fantastic average. In 1970–71 we slumped off a bit, dropping to 80 power-play goals in 78 games, and in 1971–72 we dropped to 74 power-play goals in 78 games. I may have used the wrong word by saying "dropped"; in fact, we led the NHL in power-play goals those two years and those totals rank Number 2 and Number 3 in the record books. At the same time, Phil Esposito set an NHL record in 1970–71 when he scored 25 power-play goals, then promptly broke the record the following season by scoring 28 power-play goals. The key to a successful power-play attack is the familiarity among the members of the power play. It is a matter of record that from 1967–1968 through 1971–72—a period of five years in which we won two Stanley Cups and twice finished in first place—the Bruins kept their power play practically intact. Esposito centered the forward line and had Johnny Bucyk and scrappy Johnny "Pie" McKenzie on his wings. Fred Stanfield, a center with strong puckhandling talents and a low, accurate shot that made for good deflections and good rebounds, played the left point, and I played my normal right point position. Then in 1972–73 Ken Hodge replaced McKenzie, who had signed with the new World Hockey Association, on the right wing, and several players began to alternate with Stanfield on the left point. Not surprisingly, these changes interrupted the patterned flow that we had established and refined over a five-year period, and the production of our power play slumped dramatically. However, in 1973–74 we once again led the NHL in power-play production, with Bucyk, Esposito, and Hodge working compatibly up front and Carol Vadnais, an offensive defenseman with an outstanding shot and superior puckhandling skills, joining me back at the point. I don't want to knock anyone, but I much prefer having a defenseman such as Vadnais working alongside me at the point, for obvious reasons. A defenseman is used to playing defense, so he is not about to panic if the opposition happens to break up our power play and skate back down the ice on a two-on-one against him. And he also is more accustomed to taking the puck off the boards, which is not as easy as it looks, believe me.

On our power play we always look for the open man, controlling the puck with a series of passes until one player works himself into the open. The opposition usually employs the so-called box defense against our power play; that is, the four rival players set up a square in front of their goaltender, with each individual assigned to cover a particular area. Penetrating the box formation is not easy, which explains why we oftentimes will pass the puck for thirty, sixty or even ninety seconds before taking a shot at the goaltender. When I get the puck, I am always conscious of a few things. I know that Bucyk will be stationed at his familiar position to the right of the goaltender, close enough to him to be his Siamese twin. I also know that Esposito will be roaming around in the slot, ready to deflect a shot, take a pass, or screen the goaltender's view. If there's an opening between my position and Bucyk's, I will try to get him the puck. If Esposito is free in the slot, I will either pass the puck to him or shoot it toward the net so he can deflect it en route. Then again, maybe there's an opening for me to shoot the puck myself. I do whatever my instinct tells me—and try not to panic. Two minutes is a long time. Listen. If a player can't get himself into the open at least once during a two-minute power play, well, he does not deserve to be out there when his team has that man advantage. All this talk about control, and I remember one night there was a penalty called on the opposition and two seconds later Esposito scored a goal right off the ensuing face-off. Great puck control!

**Breaking in against
Eddie Giacomin.**

CHAPTER SIX
Defense

For me, the best defense is a good offense, though I'm certain that among the hockey purists who would disagree are the goaltenders who have played behind me in Boston. In their minds, the best offense is a good defense. If I wore a mask and had pucks flying at me all night, I'd probably feel the same way. I know I've always driven the Bruins' goaltenders nuts with my particular approach to the defensive part of hockey. For years Eddie Johnston and Gerry Cheevers got hoarse yelling at me during a game:

"Look out, Bobby."

"Behind you."

"In the corner, Bobby."

"Over there, Bobby."

"Here they come."

"Pass-out, Bobby."

"Guy on the wing."

"Get out of my line, Bobby."

"Loose puck."

"Watch it, Bobby."

My problem as a defenseman is that I don't pay enough attention to the rival players standing around the net in front of my own goaltender. I'm offensive minded. I want the puck. So I'm always trying to guess where it will come out next instead of paying strict attention to those players around my net who might soon be getting a pass or a rebound. Opponents tend to sneak around me and to establish permanent stands all around my net. In the end, I get myself into a lot of trouble. I ought to start hitting and whacking those loiterers around—legally of course—just to let them know I haven't forgotten about them.

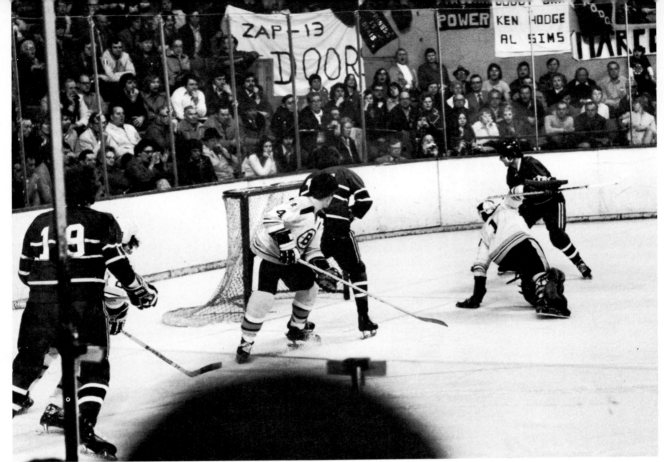

This is a classic example of a defenseman — me — being caught out of position. For some unexplainable reason, two Canadiens are suddenly closer to the Boston goal than any of the Bruins on the ice. I should have been positioned between the Montreal players, but I wasn't — and the result of this mistake should have been an easy goal for the Canadiens.

The cardinal rule for a defenseman is to always remain between the rival players and his own goaltender; in other words, the goaltender should never come face to face with an opponent. Unfortunately, this is the defensive rule I probably violate the most. My defensive game is based on the elements of risk and surprise; I'll take risks to surprise a puck carrier, and hope to get the puck from him as a result. Sometimes my gambles work, other times they fail. One night we were playing the Rangers and Gilles Gilbert, our new goaltender, had a shutout working while we were piling up a big score at the opposite end. I got too careless on defense, and I let Steve Vickers of the Rangers set up light housekeeping at the edge of the crease to Gilbert's right. Vickers is one of the many forwards in the NHL who scores probably 75 percent of his goals on plays around the goal mouth. I should have removed him from the play in some legal manner, but unfortunately I didn't. Suddenly the puck got behind me, rolled to Vickers, and poor Gilbert never had a chance. I felt foolish. Here we were attacking practically at will down the other end of the ice, and the first time my goaltender needed some help to preserve his shutout, I let him down.

In my years with the Bruins we always have been known more

for our GF records than our GA totals. GF in the daily hockey standings in your local newspaper means Goals For, while GA means Goals Against. From 1967–68 through 1973–74 the Bruins led the NHL each season in Goals For; in fact, in 1970–71 we set a league record by scoring 399 goals in 78 games, more than five goals per game. Never did we lead the NHL in Goals Against, but our cumulative total for seven years ranked Number 5 in the league. Over that same seven-season period the total difference between our Goals For and our Goals Against was easily the highest in the NHL; indeed, we scored some 750 more goals than we gave up. During those years we won more games and lost fewer than any other NHL club. So, despite the common complaint that the Bruins could not spell the word D-E-F-E-N-S-E, let alone play it, we must have been doing something right.

Our goaltenders completely understood that we were basically a high-powered scoring machine and, as a result, brought a philosophic approach to their work. They knew they would get four or five goals for a cushion each game, and it was better than playing

Goaltenders bail many a defenseman out of trouble.

those nerve-racking 1 to 0, 2 to 1, and 3 to 2 games every night. Cheevers used to keep track of unusual statistics, and one year he figured out that more than 50 percent of the opposition's goals were scored *after* we had piled up a lead of two or more goals. Johnston once said, "It's pretty hard to keep up your defensive interest when you're always ahead by a bunch of goals in the third period."

Of course, we never would have set all those goal-scoring records if we didn't have the puck, and the way we got the puck was by taking it from the opposition. How? By playing defense. By forechecking. By backchecking. By talking. By bodychecking. By blocking shots. By winning face-offs. By killing penalties. By sound work in our zone. And, at times, by fighting. As a defensive team, the Bruins play with an approach based on a certain amount of gambling inside *our* attacking zone. If an Esposito or a Sheppard, say, figures he has a 75 percent chance of taking the puck from the puck carrier with a quick poke check or sweep check, he probably will take that chance. If he gets the puck, we may score a goal. If not, the opposition may go down the ice and score. We all take those chances freely—and, as the records prove, we succeed far more often than we fail.

Defense should be a six-man effort

Defense always should be a six-man team effort, not something restricted to the two defensemen and the goaltender. Most NHL teams no longer determine the effectiveness of a forward strictly on the basis of his goals and assists. They keep something called a "Plus and Minus" record that works as a fairly accurate measure of a player's net worth. With the Bruins, if I happen to be on the ice when we score a goal while the teams are playing at equal strength, I get a "plus one" on the ledger. However, if I happen to be on the ice when the opposition scores a goal while the teams are at equal strength, I get a "minus one." Whenever I have a so-called "minus game," I know I have not played very well.

One problem with this system is that too many coaches of kids' teams forget to weigh the respective duties of their players properly as they analyze the plus and minus totals. For example, Don Marcotte plays left wing on our checking line; consequently, he usually spends all his time checking the Yvan Cournoyers, Rod Gilberts, Jimmy Pappins, René Roberts, Bill Fletts, and

Mickey Redmonds. Hazardous work, you might say, for those players are going to score their goals no matter what a checker does to them, just as Phil Esposito scores goals despite the close attention he gets from rival checkers. So in Marcotte's case, the plus and minus total can often be misleading; he could finish the year with, say, a minus ten and still have had a tremendous season. Marcotte, though, usually ends up with a "plus" total, and I'm certain that he uses it as an effective bargaining point at contract time.

Checking

Too many players in the NHL play with the misguided notion that checking is something you do only at the bank. Checking is the fundamental concept on which the entire system of defense is built. If the checking system breaks down, the opposition will tear down-ice on breakaway plays, two-on-ones, three-on-ones, three-on-twos, and every other way. A good checking team will harass the opposition into making mistakes at the worst possible moments and generally disrupt the attacking pattern to the point where it becomes disorganized confusion.

The Chicago Black Hawks, who are easily the best checkers in the NHL, often check so closely, they almost follow us to our dressing room between periods. For years the Black Hawks concentrated solely on the attacking side of hockey, and at the end of each season they usually came away with an armful of individual and team scoring records. They also came away empty-handed in the final standings and later in the play-offs, usually getting bumped out in the opening round. So in 1969 Coach Billy Reay ordered the Hawks to abandon their one-way, all-attacking game and concentrate on checking the opposition into the ice. "The better you check," Reay reasoned, "the more you will win." I remember that Bobby Hull, who had scored 58 goals the previous season to set an NHL record, was pretty upset at Reay's decision to change Chicago's style of play. Bobby figured that Reay wanted to reduce him to a simple backchecking left wing who might score 23 goals a year. Almost overnight, the Hawks went from a high-scoring team to a low-scoring band of checkers, and at the same time they cut their Goals Against totals drastically. Not coincidentally, they also finished in first place in their division for four straight years and twice advanced to the final round of the Stanley Cup play-offs.

And what about Hull? Well, Bobby still scored his 50 or so goals each year—even after he jumped to the World Hockey Association—and discovered that the checking-style hockey actually was physically easier for him. "I don't roam around the ice all the time any more," Bobby once told me. "I cover my wing, check my guys, and let things fall where they may. I used to think that my legs would give out on me before I reached the age

A

Phil Esposito does it all for the Bruins — he's not just a great goal scorer. Here Phil forechecks against defenseman Serge Savard of the Canadiens (A), closes off Savard's intended route to our zone (B), and forces him to start the Montreal breakout play all over again (C).

of thirty-eight, but now I feel as though I can play until I'm forty-five." Oddly enough, when Bobby signed with the Winnipeg Jets, he also became their coach, and now Coach Hull has his players checking first and scoring second, too. So let's examine the various types of checking tactics the Bruins use in every game.

Forechecking: Stated simply, forechecking means containing the opposition inside its own defensive zone by swarming around the puck carrier and sealing off his escape routes. It is a risky business, though, because if that puck carrier can elude the forecheckers either by making a pass or skating around them, then his team will skate down-ice with a definite manpower advantage. To minimize the risks, we never send more than two forwards in deep on our forechecking maneuvers. The wingman on the side farthest away from the puck always stays back to guard against possible disaster. As a defenseman, I am part of the second line of forechecking; the forwards represent the first line and, as such, do most of the work. Some NHL forwards, like Dennis Hextall of Minnesota and Ivan Boldirev of Chicago, prefer to forecheck the puck carrier with their body and try to take him out of the play. Other forwards, like Bobby Clarke of Philadelphia, Walt Tkaczuk of the New York Rangers, and Don Luce of Buffalo, forecheck with their body *and* their stick, sort of tattooing the puck carrier. And there are other forwards, like Dave Keon and Norm Ullman of the Toronto Maple Leafs, who

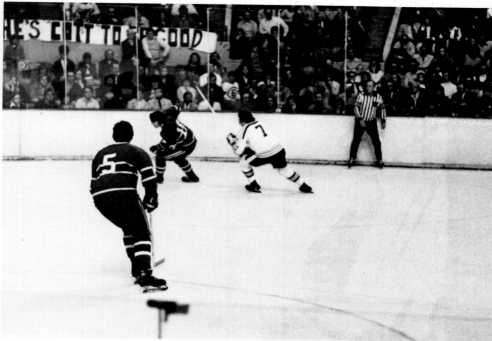

B

C

rely primarily on deft moves of their stick, sweep checks or poke checks, to disturb the rival puck carrier. The best forecheckers rarely, if ever, confront the puck carrier head-on; instead, they try to approach him at some angle in order to reduce his breakout options. And they never, never chase the puck carrier around the net or let the puck carrier get ahead of them.

When I participate actively in our forechecking plays, I generally use my stick more than my body—for safety reasons. If I miss with a poke check or a sweep check, I still can turn around and skate back into the play, but if I miss with a body check, I probably will be flat on the ice or bouncing off the boards very soon, out of the play.

A *poke check* is just that: a one-handed poke at the puck with my stick. In lining up for a poke check, I don't watch the puck as much as I watch the puck carrier's chest. If his chest is in front of me, the puck will be right below me. Even If I miss the puck with my stick, I most likely will hit the puck carrier's stick and disrupt his movement at least temporarily.

A *sweep check* also is a one-handed maneuver. Sometimes I try to sweep the puck from the puck carrier and slide it back toward me; to do this (remember, I sweep-check by holding the stick with my right hand), I sweep the blade of the stick from right to left and try to hook the puck away from him. Other times I just try to knock the puck off his stick with either a forehand or a backhand sweep. In sweep-checking, I always keep my eyes riveted

Poke checking the puck away
from Jacques Lemaire of the
Canadiens.

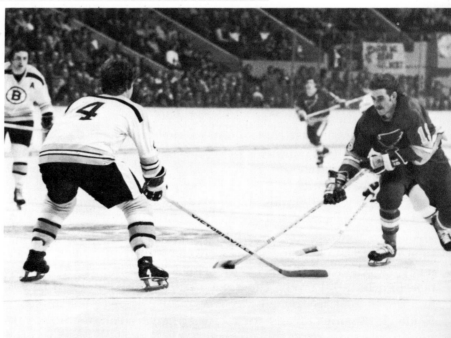

on my opponent's chest—not his eyes—then lean forward and down to execute the check. Sweep checks are riskier than poke checks, so I never sweep-check unless I feel certain that I will dislodge the puck from the carrier's stick. When poke-checking or sweep-checking, I always hold my stick as tightly as possible with my right hand. I have seen many players cost their team a goal by losing control of their stick while trying to poke-check or sweep-check the puck.

Backchecking: Once the opposition manages to elude the fore-checkers and break from its zone with the puck, we switch to backchecking. This is something forwards do more than defensemen. Most times, of course, a defenseman skates backward and faces the attack head-on. The best backcheckers—players such as Don Marcotte of the Bruins, Cliff Koroll of Chicago, Eddie Westfall of the New York Islanders, and Claude Larose of Montreal—all skate like mad, keep their opponent against the boards, and position themselves between him and wherever the puck is. And they worry primarily about their opponent, not about the puck. In backchecking I try to skate either alongside my rival or a half-stride ahead of him. Never let an opponent skate ahead of you while you are backchecking, because he would be able to put on a burst of speed and cut back in front of you to take a lead pass from a teammate. If I can keep my opponent behind me and against the boards, there is no way he can score a goal, or even make a good play. If he gets ahead of me and skates inside, then

A broad sweep check hooks the puck away from one of the St. Louis Blues.

I probably will cost my team a goal. When backchecking, I also try to bug my opponents. I lift their sticks, or maybe I rap my own stick against their pads, anything to distract them. Sometimes I even talk to them. Nothing too serious or too profound, mind you. I just ask them how the family is these days, and ask them to say hello for me.

Talking: Some players call this intimidation. Call it what you want, but it works in a lot of cases, and fails in others. On the ice I normally don't say very much to anyone, except when I am backchecking, and even then I keep my words to a minimum and try to use proper English and good grammar. Verbal intimidation *is* part of the game of hockey, however, just like physical intimidation. When we sit on our bench, we always yell things at rival players in an attempt to take their mind off the game and get them thinking about something else. If some rival thinks for a moment that a man on our team is about to get him in some way, well, that opponent no doubt will be worried more about the possibility of a physical confrontation than his backchecking duties.

Gerry Cheevers loved to ride rival players from our bench. He used to tell defensemen, "Look out, Esposito's going to fake you out next." He might simply remind them that their team was losing by three goals and they had been on the ice for every one of our goals. I remember one game against Buffalo when Gerry's remarks from the bench directly contributed to one of our goals. We had just scored on a power play while Eddie Shack of the Sabres was in the penalty box, and as Shack lined up for the face-off on his next appearance, Cheevers yelled to him: "Thanks Shackie, we couldn't have scored that last goal without your help." Shack was understandably furious, and, sure enough, ten seconds later he was back in the penalty box for tripping one of our players. We scored another power-play goal shortly afterward.

Not surprisingly, one of the chief targets of the mouthcheckers is Yvan Cournoyer, the Roadrunner of the Canadiens. Cournoyer is probably the fastest skater in the NHL, and also is one of the smallest players in the league. One night in Montreal, Glen Sather, who played for the Bruins at the time, casually warned Cournoyer: "Don't touch the puck again, or I'll knock you into the third row of the seats." Yvan laughed. "You've got to catch me first, and that you cannot do," he said to Sather. Another time, in the final game of the 1973 Stanley Cup play-offs, Cournoyer and Jerry "King-Kong" Korab of the Black Hawks were lined up for a face-off, and Korab, who at six feet four inches and two hundred and fifteen pounds dwarfed the five-foot-seven-inch, hundred-and-seventy-pound Cournoyer, said to Yvan: "Hey, what are you going to be when you grow up?" Cournoyer glared at the menacing-looking Korab and said quickly: "Something you're never going to be, a goal scorer." Moments later, Cournoyer

Body checking is just that: checking the player's body. You don't have to crash your opponent into the second row of the seats — just slide your body in his way, as I am doing here against Frank Mahovlich of the Canadiens, and keep him away from the puck.

scored the goal that won the cup for the Canadiens, then he supposedly said to Korab: "Do you want me to give you some lessons?" Even Korab had to laugh.

Bodychecking: Without doubt, bodychecking is the most misunderstood part of hockey. Ask a teenage hockey player what a bodycheck is, and he will answer that it means crashing an opponent through the boards or catapulting him into the air. A bodycheck, he'll say, is something that draws ooohs and gasps from the crowd. Listen. Bodychecking simply means getting your body into another player's way and removing him from the flow of play. I can count on one hand the number of times I have checked another player through the boards or flipped him over my shoulder. All I ever try to do is *check* the movement of my opponent's body. If I can position myself even slightly in his way, I will change his direction or stop him. Look at it this way. If I bodycheck a rival player violently into the boards or flip him

There's nothing quite like a hip check to slow down an attacker and remove him from the play. Although it looks as if Dallas Smith hit one of the Canadiens with an illegal leg check, Dallas actually caught him with a solid hip check and is in the process of regaining his balance.

Good position: I have moved to the inside of Jean Ratelle, the puck carrier, and should be able to take the puck away from him.

through the air, I most likely will remove myself from the play for several seconds. However, if I bodycheck him by just getting into his way, I will remain in the play and perhaps help prevent a goal.

When I bodycheck, I try to position my body so that if I miss my opponent, I will not suddenly find myself either flat on the ice or careening toward the boards. To check with my body, I again train my eyes on the chest of my opponent—he must move where his chest moves, remember—and try to put my shoulder squarely into his chest. Believe me, a shoulder stuck into a player's chest will do the trick every time. Perhaps the most glamorous of all bodychecks is the *hip check*, since the recipient usually ends up doing a triple somersault through the air before crashing to the ice. Leo Boivin, a short, stocky defenseman, was a great hip-checker before he retired a few years ago; Leo used to crouch

Familiarity breeds success on defense. Dale Rolfe (5) and Brad Park (2) have been defense partners in New York for several seasons and they understand each other's every move. Here Ken Hodge tries to cut between Rolfe and Park (A), but they quickly close the opening (B) and sandwich Hodge to a stop (C) before Park skates off to pick up the puck (D).

low, skate either backward or sideward at the unsuspecting puck carrier, and then catch him with an outstretched hip and flip him into the air. One of the NHL's best hip checkers now is Ron Harris of the New York Rangers. Like Boivin, Harris is built like a fire hydrant and starts his devastating hip checks from practically ice level. It was Harris, remember, who caught Phil Esposito with a great hip check in the 1973 Stanley Cup play-offs and sent Phil to the hospital for knee surgery. Harris was not running wildly at Esposito; he happened to hit Phil with a perfectly clean check at the right moment. In fact, Harris was down so low when he came at Phil that I don't think Phil ever saw him until it was too late.

But no matter how diligently my teammates forecheck at the other end of the ice, the opposition certainly will break out at times and press the attack. In all these typical confrontations I am about to describe, I always forget my offensive inclinations and stick strictly to my defensive duties.

Tactics

One-on-One: A defenseman should win this *mano-a-mano* battle ninety-nine times out of a hundred. By winning, I simply mean that my goaltender and I combine to prevent the puck carrier from scoring a goal. As a rule, the attacking player is skating

C

D

forward with the puck out in front of him, while I am skating backward and facing the puck carrier head-on. Under no circumstances do I want the puck carrier to get between me and my goaltender; indeed, that is always suicidal. In these situations I forget about the puck because I instinctively know where it is—that is, right there on his stick. I also forget about the puck carrier's eyes and shoulders and hips and knees. Instead, I look him squarely in the chest—no place else—and try to eliminate him from the play. To do this, I brake my backward motion and stick my shoulder into his chest. I never, never try to take an opponent out with a hip check or some other type of low check in these situations because it is much easier for a player to avoid a hip than a shoulder. However, oftentimes the puck carrier will anticipate this maneuver and try to cross me up by shooting the puck. If this happens, I will either poke my stick at the puck in an attempt to dislodge or deflect it, or else I will drop down to block the shot. Throughout the entire one-on-one maneuver, I also try to force the puck carrier off to a bad shooting angle, preferably on his backhand side. Do I try to outguess the puck carrier on these plays? Never. Try to outguess a Cournoyer moving toward you at full speed, and you will pay the price. Finally, if the puck carrier happens to beat you cleanly and is moving in alone against your goaltender, don't worry about taking him

down with an accidental-looking trip or an innocent-looking hook. A penalty beats a goal every time.

Two-on-One: Double trouble. With the Bruins we have an unwritten rule that the defenseman is primarily responsible for the man *without* the puck and the goaltender is responsible for the player *with* the puck. While this approach may not sound very sensible, it is extremely logical. Think of it this way. By covering the man without the puck, I eliminate one of the two attackers from the play and leave my goaltender with only one player—the

Carol Vadnais has established perfect position on this play as he forces the New York player away from the net and the puck so Terry O'Reilly (24) can skate in and collect the rebound. On two-on-one plays, remember that the goaltender is responsible for the shooter and the lone defenseman is responsible for the other attacker.

puck carrier—to worry about. On the other hand, if I go out to play the puck carrier, my goaltender then must worry about two possibilities: (1) the puck carrier may shoot the puck; or (2) the puck carrier may fake a shot and pass the puck to his uncovered teammate, who most likely will have a wide-open net at which to shoot. On these plays I stay between the two attackers as they skate down the ice and keep my stick full-extended in front of me; by doing that, I may be able to deflect an opponent's pass or shot. While my responsibility may concern the player without the

puck, I don't completely ignore the puck carrier; in fact, I'm not going to let him skate right in on my goaltender for an easy shot from a good angle. Here I rely on my instinct again—and then react accordingly. If it appears to me that the puck carrier will forget his teammate and fire the puck at my goaltender, I will quickly move toward him and try to deflect the puck with my stick or block it with my body.

Two-on-Two: Simple, although nothing really is simple in hockey. Basically, each defenseman is responsible for an attacking player, in most cases the opponent skating on his side of the ice. Like the one-on-one, the defending team should win these confrontations ninety-nine times out of a hundred. On these plays the defensemen should hold the attacking players out away from the goal and reduce their shooting angle to zero. The one thing I have noticed most about young defensemen is that they back in too much on their goaltender, thus enlarging the shooter's target and at times screening their goaltender's vision. In working against the two-on-two, I always have it in my mind that I don't want the play to become a two-on-one; in other words, I handle it straight and try to remove my man from the play.

Three-on-Two: Dallas Smith may be the most underrated defenseman in hockey. We worked as a regular defense team for more than six years, and during that time we established a solid rapport—almost a mental telepathy—that enabled us to handle plays such as the three-on-two with a minimum of confusion. Once the attacking team breaks in on a three-on-two play, the defensemen should stagger themselves slightly according to the position of the attacking puck carrier. For example, I play the right defense. If the rival left wing is carrying the puck down my side of the ice on a three-on-two play, I stay slightly in front of my defense partner as we skate backward and try to force that puck carrier into taking a shot from a bad angle or making a pass. Meanwhile, my defense partner behind me should react in the direction of any pass and get into position to block a follow-up shot or another pass. If the rival right wing is carrying the puck, I stay back and let my defense partner stay up. If the rival center happens to be carrying the puck down the middle, we play it by instinct. In these situations the center usually will shoot the puck, so we try to clog his shooting lanes and force him to make a pass.

Three-on-One: Disaster. This is when I pray for help and hope that one or more of my teammates is coming back down the ice to give me some help. The defenseman usually is at the mercy of the attackers on a three-on-one play. I simply try to stay in the middle and force the attackers to spread out. Then I pray that my goaltender will make a great save. As a rule, defensemen lose this battle about 60 percent of the time, although I don't like to call it a personal loss. Anytime the opposition skates down-ice

Dallas Smith (20) and Carol Vadnais (10) demonstrate the perfect staggered position while defending against a three-on-two play.

with a three-on-one, it means that at least two of my teammates have been caught up the ice. They gambled, and lost. I remember watching a kids' game one night when a coach berated this ten- or eleven-year-old defenseman for not stopping a three-on-one, and the kid was so upset by the criticism that he did nothing right the rest of the game. Listen. Show me a defenseman who stops three-on-one plays all the time, and I'll show you a miracle man. That coach should have blamed the players who were caught up-ice and, in effect, created the three-on-one play for the opposition.

Shot Blocking

As I have indicated, many times the best way to handle a direct confrontation with a shooter is by trying to block his shot with your body before it ever gets to the goaltender. Shot blocking understandably is a tricky maneuver—and extremely hazardous.

Don't drop all the way down to a shot unless you need to. Try to stay on your feet and get as close to the shooter as possible (left). By keeping on your feet, you are prepared to chase the rebounding puck (right).

It also requires perfect timing. When I block a shot, I drop down to one knee—never two knees—and attempt to smother the puck with my chest. By dropping down on only one knee, not two, I find it much easier to get back onto my feet and back into the play in the event that I have just redirected the puck rather than smothered it. However, I never drop down to block any shot unless I am within five feet of the puck. For two reasons: If I go down too soon, the shot will have more than enough time to rise up and crash into my face. Second, if I go down too soon, the shooter can fake a shot, collect the puck, and skate around me for a closer and undoubtedly better shot at my goaltender. Right, Yvan? In my rookie season Yvan Cournoyer gave me his big windup and all his facial grimaces, so I went down to block his shot. Before I knew it, Cournoyer had gone around me with the puck, and he beat our goaltender cleanly. Needless to say, I felt stupid. Like a rookie.

211

The other basic shot-blocking technique is the *sliding block*, something that Don Awrey, formerly of the Bruins and now with St. Louis, has perfected. Once Awrey is 100 percent certain that a player will shoot the puck and not pass it, he slides feetfirst at the puck like a base runner sliding into second base. As he slides toward the puck, Awrey keeps his feet together and gets his head out of the way. This is a very effective tactic *if* — and I can't stress too much the importance of that *if* — the shooter does in fact shoot the puck. Once a defenseman slides toward the puck, he has totally committed himself to a specific maneuver. If the shot becomes a fake, then the sliding defenseman is in trouble.

Defensive Don'ts

As you read some of the No-Nos I am about to discuss, I'm sure you are going to say to yourself: "How come Orr can do some of the things he is telling me I should never do?" At times I do violate some of the basic rules of playing defense, but I never violate any rule unless I feel that I have a 100 percent chance of getting away with it. And, remember, I play hockey every day for a living, while you are out there for fun and recreation and a little competition perhaps two or three days a week.

—Don't play with the puck in your own zone. Get it out of trouble as quickly as possible, particularly if you are the final line of protection for your goaltender.

—Don't stickhandle in your own zone unless one of your team-mates is nearby and in good position to take a pass in case of trouble.

—Don't skate in front of your net with the puck.

—Don't pass the puck across the front of your net.

—Don't screen your goaltender from the puck.

—Don't leave your goaltender naked; that is, don't leave him all alone, without any protection, in front of the net.

—Don't let rival players set up residence around the front of your net, something I let happen too often.

Strangely enough, one way to prevent those opponents from establishing good position around the net is by cheating. A smart

By stationing myself between the two attacking Rangers on this two-on-one play, I managed to force Jim Neilson to the outside for a shot on Gilles Gilbert. Gilbert had moved out to cut down the angle, and he handled Neilson's shot by making a good save with his pads. The rebound was almost directly behind me and I had to hustle to knock it away from the charging Ratelle.

defenseman should be able to hide the fact that he is holding—or otherwise interfering with—a rival player in front of the net, although holding has become more difficult to conceal now that NHL rules force defensemen to wear gloves *with* uncut palms. For years defensemen used to wear gloves without palms, and they could camouflage all the holding they did around the net. It is also useful to harass your opponent both verbally and with your stick. No player likes to get rapped around the ankles with the blade of a stick, but if an opponent wants to stand around the front of my net, he should pay the price. A black-and-blue price, mind you. Poor Phil Esposito. They hold him. They shove him. They whack him in the ankles, the arms, the chest, the back, the head, the knees. Everywhere. Still, they only tattoo Phil's body and leave him black and blue, while he leaves them red-faced with embarrassment by scoring goal after goal after goal and wearing out that red bulb behind the poor goaltenders. Other

How to get a penalty: hold the attacking player, as I am doing to Ted Irvine of the Rangers (left) and Mickey Redmond of the Red Wings (bottom). As I have learned, you can't fool the referees too often in a game.

The goal-mouth battles are rugged during a game. Trying to muscle Walter Tkaczuk out of the play (left) is like trying to move a five-hundred-pound boulder. On the right, Brad Park and I are locked in a struggle for position. He seems to be annoyed about something.

players, though, hardly accept love taps to the ankle the way Esposito does, and it is easy to move them away from the net and out of harm's way. Come to think of it, I really must start getting tougher with opponents who like to hang around our net.

Penalty Killing

There are two ways to approach the art of penalty killing: (1) the Boston way, or (2) the NHL way. In Boston we operate on the theory that playing shorthanded creates an ideal situation for us to try to score a goal, too. The other teams in the NHL, though, seem to think that penalty killing simply means absorbing a two-minute penalty without making any conscious goal-scoring attempts of their own. For years Derek Sanderson and Eddie Westfall were the penalty-killing specialists for the Bruins, and they were without doubt the best penalty-killing unit in hockey. When they were on the ice while we were shorthanded, I always felt that our chances for scoring a goal were at least as good as the team with the power play. In fact, thanks mostly to Sanderson and Westfall, the Bruins hold the top two places in the NHL record book with 25 shorthanded goals in 1970–71 and 18 shorthanded goals in 1971–72. Now Phil Esposito, Gregg Shep-

pard, and Don Marcotte are the penalty-killing specialists for the Bruins, and they all operate on that same theory.

The system employed by Walt Tkaczuk and Bill Fairbairn of the New York Rangers, another one of the best penalty-killing teams in the NHL, contrasts with our Bruin approach. Once Tkaczuk or Fairbairn gets the puck, the Rangers try to control play by either skating around center ice or making passes. Occasionally they do score a goal, but they think more about playing keepaway with the puck than shooting it past the opposition goaltender.

I prefer the Boston approach because the odds become very interesting. You must remember that most power plays feature a forward playing one of the defense positions, and these forwards don't know how to handle a one-on-one or a two-on-one break against them because they rarely encounter such situations under normal circumstances. So if their regular defenseman on the power play gets trapped too deep in the attacking zone, we always try to bust a Sheppard or an Esposito down-ice against that forward who is playing out of position. In other words, we try to create a total mismatch. Esposito particularly likes to work on that forward who happens to be playing defense on the power play. Phil is a superior penalty killer; in fact, he claims jokingly that penalty killing provides him with his *only* chance to look spectacular. Once Phil collects the puck, he checks the clock and begins to skate up-ice, circling around to avoid opponents, wasting time, and acting as though he were in no great rush to go anywhere. All the time he is moving forward—slowly, perhaps, but forward—and getting ready to break quickly on a surprise attack once an opening presents itself.

Still, there are many occasions when we must tend to our strict defensive duties while killing our penalties. Like all clubs, we employ the standard "box" defense in front of our goaltender when the opposition has a six-man to five-man advantage and the standard "triangle" defense when the opposition has a six-man to four-man advantage. The box is just that, with the two defensemen staying back near the goaltender and the two forwards standing up front. The trick is to stay patient and not abandon the box while the other club is moving the puck around and around in search for the supposed open man. The box normally is difficult to penetrate, and players shooting from outside the box usually will not have much of an angle at the net. We use the "triangle" when we are two men down. In this defense, two defensemen stay back and the lone forward operates out in front of them, moving from side to side with the movement of the puck but never, never abandoning his basic position.

Personally, I have two favorite penalty-killing tactics. The first is very simple: I skate behind my net with the puck and stand there as long as the opposition will let me. When they send

When shorthanded and double-teamed behind your own net, it is often best to freeze the puck and get a face-off.

221

Phil Esposito is one of the best
face-off artists in the NHL. In
this particular situation, he will
probably try to slide the puck
back toward me.

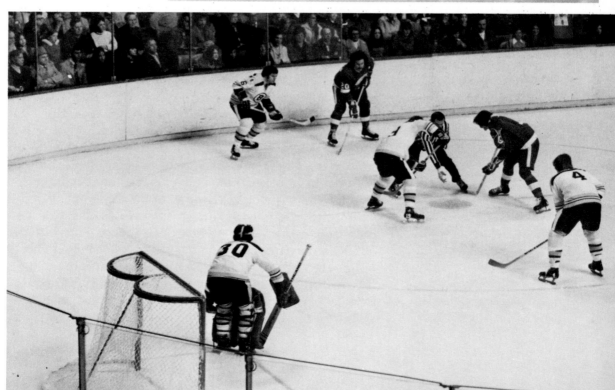

The Bruins were playing shorthanded during this face-off near the goal, so I moved into an open slot between center Gregg Sheppard and wing Don Marcotte (21). From that position I could handle any puck that went back toward the net and I could intercept any pass-out to Detroit wing Nick Libett (14).

a man after me, I will either skate out and dispose of the puck somehow or simply skate out, make my "U" turn around my goaltender, and return immediately to my starting position behind the net. The second also is pretty simple. For obvious reasons teams like to load their power play with their best goal scorers. In most cases, the best goal scorers are not exactly the best checkers. So, when I skate out of my zone with the puck, the forwards on the opposition power play usually don't check me too closely, figuring that I will skate to center ice and then dump the puck into their zone. Sure enough, I do skate to center ice—as slowly as possible, taking the longest route imaginable. Ninety feet can become three hundred and sixty feet, if I work it properly. Once at center ice, though, I don't shoot the puck into their zone; instead, I make another "U" turn and casually skate all the way back to my starting position behind my net. Meanwhile, the clock continues to tick away. If all goes well, the opposition power play will become flustered and disorganized. Then what normally happens is two members of the power play will skate behind the net—one from each side—in an attempt to take the puck away. Great! Once I see this, I either fire the puck around the boards or flip it high through the center of the ice—and out of trouble.

Face-offs

I doubt that I have taken more than a handful of face-offs in my NHL career; indeed, I much prefer to stay back and get the puck from a face-off. We have always had excellent face-off men in Boston, particularly Sanderson and Esposito. Derek will never admit it, but he psyched himself into becoming a super face-off specialist—in fact, probably the best in the league. He rarely, if ever, played on our power play, but instead of complaining about it, Derek developed superior skills in the specialty areas of killing penalties and winning face-offs. Stan Mikita of the Chicago Black Hawks was recognized as the master of the face-off circle until Derek beat him on something like twenty-seven of thirty-one face-offs in a Stanley Cup play-off game one season. For years Derek took all our important face-offs, and he usually won them. How important are face-offs? Listen to this sad story. In the 1969 Stanley Cup play-offs we played the Canadiens in the semifinal series. The first two games were played at the Forum in Montreal, and we led both games by one goal in the last minute of play. However, in both games we lost face-offs near Gerry Cheevers in that closing minute, and in both games the Canadiens promptly scored the tying goal. They ultimately won both games in overtime en route to winning the series four games to two. Jean Beliveau and Ralph Backstrom won those face-offs for the Canadiens, as I remember. Unfortunately for the Bruins, Sanderson was not on the ice for either one.

Watch Esposito on face-offs some night. To start, he looks around at each of his teammates to make sure they are in position and ready for the play. His last look always goes to the goaltender; in fact, he will never take a face-off unless the goaltender has signaled to him that he is completely prepared. He stands squarely, with feet spread wide for better balance and strength, and his body weight is up on the balls of his feet. For better stick control, he spreads his hands well apart on the handle of the stick. If Espo wants to draw the puck back to one of his defensemen, he will set his bottom (left) hand as far down the shaft of the stick as possible. Once the official drops the puck, the face-off becomes a battle of reflexes—and the man with the best technique and the best timing usually wins. The best face-off men in the NHL also study rival centers and the officials in an attempt to discover their possible weaknesses on face-offs. If a center likes to draw the puck to his right on the face-off, you can be sure that Esposito knows that and, more importantly, knows how to counteract it. There used to be a linesman in the NHL who always closed his left hand and made a fist at the precise moment he dropped the puck with his right hand. Our centers spotted the official's habit, and for a long time we didn't lose many face-offs when he dropped the puck.

Fighting

I am not quite certain whether this section on fighting should be included here in the defensive chapter or back in the attacking chapter. Despite what the purists claim, fighting *is* part of the game of hockey. Believe me, I am not a devoted advocate of the fighting approach, but the feverish pace and strong contact of a hockey game do produce fights. They are inescapable. I have won some fights, but I've lost a few dandies. In many ways, fighting is almost like shooting the puck, since I want to get as much power as possible behind my punch. To set up, I turn the blades of my skates to the outside, pointing them to about a ten minutes past ten position. By doing that, I will have better balance and probably won't slide too much. As I throw my punches, I lean forward—practically on my toes—and throw my body behind the punch. Not quite like a heavyweight champion would do it, but usually good enough on a hockey rink. Most fights, though, generally become wrestling matches, with words of wisdom passing between the opponents. In these skirmishes, I try to pull my opponent's shirt over his head. By doing that, I will block his vision and also tangle his arms straitjacket-style, which means that he will be unable to punch me. Some players, however, have solved the shirt-over-the-head dilemma by taping or tying their shirts to their uniform pants. Don't go looking for fights, but don't back away from any fights either.

224

Dave Schultz and I aren't
throwing many punches here,
but we're still headed for the
penalty box.

CHAPTER SEVEN

Coach's Corner

During the off season I spend the great majority of my time working as a hockey coach at the Orr-Walton Sports Camp in Orillia, Ontario. More than twenty-one hundred youngsters attend the camp each summer, and we have devised what I think is a model instructional program that incorporates every teaching point imaginable—and everything that I discuss in this book. By we, I mean Bill Watters, the camp director who has earned his master's degree in physical education; Mike Walton; and myself, with considerable expert assistance from the staff of professional hockey players that helps conduct the on-ice sessions. Each day we stress one particular aspect of hockey, starting, of course, with skating. And the exercises are not automatic. We always explain what a drill is and why it is important, then the professional instructors demonstrate the drill itself. I always emphasize to the youngsters that each drill actually serves as an exercise for several techniques. Take the basic figure eight drill, probably the oldest training maneuver in hockey. As I tell the young players, the figure eight is an exercise that, if properly executed, will (1) perfect a player's starting technique; (2) strengthen his skating stride; (3) perfect his difficult crossover turns *both* ways around the net; (4) develop his stamina; and (5) perfect his stopping technique. The figure eight is not simply a leisurely skate around the ice.

To me, the one unfortunate result of the historic Team Canada–Russia hockey series in 1972 was the loud complaint that Russian hockey players are in better shape than North American hockey players. In better shape for what? For playing soccer? Volleyball? Basketball? Maybe so—but not for playing hockey. The Russian players worked 90 percent harder than our skaters before the start of the series, but after a month of on-ice conditioning the Team Canada players were in a physical condition that was at least the equal of the Soviet players, if not better. By that, I mean we were in shape to play a sixty-minute hockey game at full speed.

Sure, the Russians no doubt would wallop us any day at soccer or basketball or volleyball, but they did not beat us on the ice. It's right there in the record books: Canada 4 and Russia 3, with one tie game. What is hockey condition anyway? It is an ability to perform at a peak physical and mental level during that time you are out on the ice. Not out on the soccer field or the basketball court.

The Russians force-feed sports

All things considered, I think that our sports systems hold up pretty well in the international arena. Our kids, remember, dabble in a number of sports for short periods of the year. For instance, youngsters play hockey during the winter, switch to baseball for the spring and summer, and then play football in the fall. They are getting a well-rounded athletic training. More importantly, a sport is not forced on them. The Russians, on the other hand, force-feed a particular sport to their players; in fact, a member of any Soviet national athletic team at any age level spends eleven and a half months a year in serious training for his sport. Ridiculous, if you ask me.

Personally, I believe that hockey players should conserve their energy during the long season so they will have that energy when they need it most, like in the final minutes of a hockey game. I'm afraid that the Russian experience has persuaded some NHL teams that soccer and volleyball and basketball and marathon running and exercise machines are the only way to get in shape and then stay in shape. Such training may be all right for preseason activity, and perhaps early in the regular-season schedule, but once a player has skated in eight or ten games he will have gained his hockey conditioning and will not need any other conditioning stimulants.

As I remember, two National Hockey League teams—the

Buffalo Sabres and the Detroit Red Wings—were so intrigued by the Soviet team's conditioning techniques that they promptly copied them and forced their players to spend as long as one hour each day working on what I like to call "nonhockey exercises." All the Red Wings, for instance, had to spend at least thirty minutes working on a universal exercise machine in a room near their dressing quarters. The Sabres were almost unreal. On days when they did not have to play a game, they started practice by running two or three miles around the outside of their arena or their hotel; if weather conditions were poor, they ran around the corridors of the Aud in Buffalo. After hockey practice, they went to their weight room and spent another half hour working with barbells, dumbbells and the universal machine. And the club even hired a former wrestler named Fred Atkins to lead them through special P.T. exercises both at home and on the road.

Not surprisingly, the Red Wings and the Sabres started that season with a bang and were the top teams in the NHL's East Division for almost a month. However, once the other clubs got themselves into condition the standard way—that is, by playing ten or twelve games under normal regular-season conditions—they soon caught the Wings and the Sabres. As it turned out, Detroit missed the play-offs while Buffalo made them on the final night of the season.

So I don't think we should change any of our training techniques. I do think, though, that we ought to improve the techniques we do use. And we should also use all the available ice time each day in the most efficient way. One way to do that is by using more than one puck during a practice. For instance, what we now do at all our practices in Boston is drop about twenty-five pucks at center ice or in the corner and have players repeatedly pass the puck to teammates skating toward the goaltender. We wait no more than five or six seconds between passes. So everyone is involved—and the goaltender also has to stop a shot every five or six seconds. Another thing we do is have straight ten-minute hockey games; that is, five players on each side—excluding the goaltenders—skate at full speed for ten minutes without worrying about any whistles. This type of workout develops endurance, to say the least.

Off the ice, two of the best conditioning devices are street hockey games and pure, simple running. And running. And running some more. The best thing about street hockey is that you run all the time, then must stop suddenly. Also, once you stop, you must turn immediately and start back in the opposite direction. In other words, you cannot take the tourist route and *glide* around the net. It never hurts a hockey player to run. As a youngster I ran every night during the off season, covering a course of almost four miles around the cove in Parry Sound.

Even now I still run long distances in the off-season to maintain my stamina. And I work on my sprints, too, to build up my leg muscles. I've noticed that football teams now test their players on how fast they can run the forty-yard dash—not the hundred-yard dash. Most hockey plays are like football plays: breakaway speed is considerably more important than long-distance skating or running. Think of it this way: run distances for stamina and sprints for speed. In the off-season, that is. Don't start running marathon distances or countless hundred-yard dashes during the hockey season. If you do, you will wear yourself out for hockey.

The following is a rough but basic five-day, all-purpose teaching program that can serve as a loose guide for coaches and players alike. Please remember that all drills should be structured to fit the skill level of the particular individual.

Day One

Teaching Points

Forward Skating:
    (1) your knees should be slightly bent, feet comfortably apart
    (2) start up on your toes, push off, and run for three or four steps
    (3) extend your leg completely as you stride
    (4) use both skates to stop
        — keep the skates parallel at right angles to the direction of movement
        — lean your body back
        — exert as much stopping force as possible on the outside edge of the back blade of your skate
    (5) lean toward the center to turn
        — keep your shoulders parallel to the ice
        — bend your inside knee
        — lead with your inside foot
        — pick up your outside foot and step over your inside foot
        — use a crossover step

Backward Skating:
    (1) keep your legs flexible
    (2) wiggle-waggle your hips
    (3) keep your seat over the ice
    (4) use the backward-to-forward stepover turn
    (5) practice backward stopping

Drills

    (1) figure eights (forward *and* backward)
    (2) stops and starts (blue line to blue line, also boards to boards)

When teaching skating, I emphasize bent knees, full strides, and weight well forward.

(3) backward skating (players skate backward around the face-off circles)

(4) agility skating (players change direction on instructor's whistle)

(5) striding and balance (players skate around the ice without lifting the blades of their skates off the ice)

(6) strength (one player holds his stick at shoulder level while another *pushes* and then *pulls* him around the ice, holding onto the stick)

(7) turning (tight turns around markers placed on the ice; crossover turns over the markers)

(8) defensive mobility (the instructor works closely with the defenseman, directing him here, there, everywhere with a series of hand signals)

(9) long-distance skate (ten laps around the rink; the winner gets a prize)

(10) rabbit chase (one skater gets a ten-stride lead; the first player to catch him gets a reward)

Teaching Points

Puckhandling:

(1) position your hands comfortably on the stick
(2) carry the puck in the middle of the blade
(3) carry the puck in front of you, not beside you (you can be checked from behind if you carry it on the side)
(4) keep your body between the puck and the checkers
(5) when carrying the puck around the net or a rival, lean into the turn and keep the puck away from the rival
(6) when turning with the puck, keep it on the inside of the blade—not the outside
(7) carry the puck in front of you in a comfortable position, not too far ahead of you and not too close to your feet
(8) always look ahead with your head in such a position that you can see both the puck and the man or the net in front of you

Drills

(1) keepaway (the puck carrier must remain inside the zone and keep the puck away from three checkers)
(2) figure eights (several players do figure eights with the puck on their sticks; the instructors try to poke the puck off the sticks occasionally. This exercise teaches the puckhandlers to keep their heads up)
(3) markers (the puck carrier weaves through markers set in a straight line down the ice, or he weaves slalomlike from side to side of the rink around widely set markers. Once the puckhandler loses the puck, he must start over again)
(4) breakaway (the stickhandler tries to stickhandle around the goaltender)
(5) foot drill (the players skate around the ice controlling the puck with their feet)
(6) rabbit chase (the stickhandler is chased by three checkers trying to take the puck away)

Day Three

Teaching Points

Making a Pass:

(1) always look where you are passing the puck
(2) pass the puck to the other player's stick
(3) sweep the pass, never slap it
(4) lead the receiver
(5) when passing, keep the puck in the middle of the blade
(6) when passing, point your follow-through at the player you are passing to

Receiving a Pass:
    (1) keep your stick on the ice
    (2) cup the blade of your stick
    (3) relax your lower-hand grip so that the stick gives slightly
    (4) watch the puck hit the stick
    (5) give a target, by keeping your stick on the ice

Drills

    (1) passing/receiving (two players position themselves fifteen feet apart and pass back and forth with the instructor watching closely for proper technique)
    (2) flip pass (the player must flip the puck over a stick on the ice to a teammate close by)
    (3) board work (the player angles the puck off the boards to his teammate up-ice; the player takes the pass off the boards)
    (4) drop pass (the player must leave the puck in the "dead" position)
    (5) line break (three linemates break up-ice, passing the puck constantly)
    (6) headman pass (the defensemen work long passes to breaking forwards)
    (7) give-and-go (the player stickhandles with the puck, passes it to his teammate at the boards, goes around a marker, then collects the return pass—a flip pass or a straight pass—from his teammate)

Day Four

Teaching Points

Shooting: wrist shot
    (1) position your hands comfortably on the stick
    (2) look where you are shooting
    (3) slide the puck from back to front, using the middle of your blade
    (4) shoot off your front foot
    (5) roll your wrists under—not over—as you shoot
    (6) have all your weight forward as you release the puck
    (7) for a high shot, follow through high
    (8) for a low shot, follow through low
    (9) don't lose your balance

Shooting: backhand
    (1) use the same basic principles as for the wrist shot, but keep your bottom hand a little lower on the handle

Shooting: slap shot
    (1) hold the stick firmly

This is a balance exercise we use at our hockey camp. Try standing, and skating with one knee held up by your stick.

(2) keep your bottom hand lower on the shaft than it is for the wrist shot
(3) push from the back to the front and let the puck go from the front foot
(4) bring the stick back about waist high—never over your head
(5) slap right at the puck, not behind it
(6) follow through either high or low, depending on what you want the puck to do
(7) keep your head over the puck
(8) maintain your balance

Drills

    (1) target (the players shoot at the boards to develop feel, control, and technique, under the supervision of the instructor)

    (2) flip shot (block the bottom part of the net with a board and have the player flip the puck over the board and into the net from close range)

    (3) combinations
- the player shoots immediately after a give-and-go pass play with his teammate
- the player streaks from the blue line to receive a corner pass-out and shoots on the net at the same time
- every two seconds the puck is shot toward a player standing in the slot, who must get a shot off at the goaltender

    (4) marker (the player zigzags through markers, maintaining puck control, then must shoot at the goaltender on the instructor's signal)

    (5) rabbit chase (the puck carrier must get a shot off despite harassment from a backchecker)

    (6) one-on-one (the player skates down-ice with the puck and must beat a defenseman and the goaltender with a shot or fake)

    (7) slap shot (the player slaps from both a stationary position and in full stride)

Day Five

Teaching Points

Forechecking:

    (1) play the man with the puck
    (2) make the man with the puck pass it
    (3) stay in front of the puck carrier
    (4) never chase the puck carrier behind the net; remain in front

Backchecking:

    (1) stay with the opponent all the way to the net
    (2) keep the opponent between you and the boards
    (3) worry about the check only—not the puck
    (4) harass and talk to the opponent

Poke Check:

    (1) don't watch the puck
    (2) look at the opponent's chest
    (3) remain upright
    (4) wait for the opponent to get close

Sweep Check:

    (1) use the same basic principles as for the poke check
    (2) make certain you will succeed before you try it

(3) bend your body lower to the ice

(4) keep your eye on your opponent's chest

Bodycheck:

(1) position yourself between the opponent and your goal-tender at all times

(2) study your opponent's chest

(3) don't miss!

Drills

(1) combinations
    —the player forechecks and gets the puck; the man who lost it must try to get it back by forechecking
    —the player backchecks down-ice on the opponent; then they skate around the net and reverse roles

(2) one-on-ones (*mano-a-mano* confrontations for sweep checks, poke checks, and bodychecks)

As you see, we combine as many techniques as possible into every drill. A player does not just shoot the puck. He shoots it after skating around markers, passing it off, getting it back, eluding checkers, and controlling it with his feet. Once he shoots it, he doesn't stop near the net for a rest. No. He skates off to backcheck against another player.

At the camp we spend approximately two and one-half hours a day working with the youngsters on the main teaching points scheduled for the particular group. Then the players scrimmage for twenty-five to thirty minutes under the supervision of the professional instructors, who skate along with the play and constantly comment on the things that the youngsters are doing—or not doing. After five days these youngsters may not be so many little Yvan Cournoyers or Phil Espositos, but they have had fun and they are better hockey players because they know what they are doing on the ice and why they are doing it.

A group of my young Boston friends.

Picture Credits

Dick Raphael for *Sports Illustrated: Cover*
Melchior Di Giacomo for *Sports Illustrated: 55, 82*
John Hanlon for *Sports Illustrated: 143*
Tony Triolo for *Sports Illustrated: 128, 129, 140, 182, 217*
Tom Ettinger: *12, 15, 16, 17, 18, 20, 26, 34, 145, 162*
Courtesy Mr. and Mrs. Doug Orr: *14, 21, 22, 29, 30, 37*
Ray Lussier for the *Boston Herald American/Advertiser* © 1970: *45*

All other photography by Heinz Kluetmeier

Design by Irwin Glusker